श्री ललिता सहस्त्रनाम स्त्रोत्रम्
Sri Lalita Sahasranama Stotram

श्री ललिता सहस्त्रनाम स्त्रोत्रम्

Sri Lalita Sahasranama Stotram

(Thousand Attributes of Para Shakti Lalita)
(Text with Interpretive Translation from Kashmir Sakta Viewpoint)

Dr. Chaman Lal Raina

SHARADA

Sharada Publishing House
Delhi - 110035
2000

First Published 2000
ISBN : 81-85616-28-0

Published by :
B.L. Bansal
SHARADA PUBLISHING HOUSE
40, Anand Nagar, Inderlok,
Delhi - 110035. Tel. : 5117390

Laser Typesetting by :
Sri Balaji Computers
4615/13, Tri Nagar, Delhi-35
Ph. : 7108270

Printed at :
Santosh Offset
Delhi-110 035

Dedicated to my Mother
SHOBHA
Who Taught me
the Alphabets of
SRI VIDYA

ध्यानम्

सिन्दूरारूणविग्रहां त्रिणयनां माणिक्य मौलिस्फुरत्
तारानायक शेखरां स्मितमुखीमापीनवक्षोरुहाम् ।
पाणिम्यामलिपूर्णरत्नचषकं रक्तोत्मलं बिभ्रतीं
सौम्यां रत्नघटस्थरक्तचरणां ध्यायेत्परामम्बिकाम् ।।

Sindura'runa-vigraham trinayanam manikya-mauli-sphurat,
tara-nayaka-sekharam smita-mukhim apina-Vaksoruham
Panibhyam alipurna-ratna-casakam raktopalam-bibhratim
Saumyam ratna-ghatastha-rakta-caranam dhyaget param ambikam

"I bow and surrender to her feet and take refuge in her, who has three eyes; her hue is like that of red 'Sindura'. She wears the diadem of precious stones and a crescent is shining wonderfully on it. She is easily accessible with her benign smile. Her children get an inexhaustible store of 'life-milk' in her full breast. She has vessel of honey in one hand and the red lotus in the other. It symbolises joy and wisdom. Her feet is placed on the precious pot full of valuable gems indicating that she is easily attained."

श्रीचक्रम्

बिन्दुत्रिकोणवसुकोणदशारयुग्म मन्वश्रनागदल संयुतषोडश्मरम्।
वृत्रयं च धरणीसदनत्रयं व श्रीचक्रमेतदुदितं परदेवतायाः।।

Sricakram

bindu-trikona-vasu-kona-dasara-yugma-manvasra-naga-dala-samyuta-sodasaram
Vrtta-trayam ca dharani-sadana trayam ca Sricakrametaduditam para-devatayah

PREFACE

A nice exposition of the devotional philosophy is found in the 'Sri Lalitasahsranama Stotram'. The Supreme Mother Lalita is adored with the thousand divine Names, Conveying a 'journey of Consciousness' from Sri Mata to 'Sri Lalitambika'. This is a highly occult Shakta Scripture and forms a section of the 'Brahmanda Purana'; and is regarded as the most sacred text by the followers of 'Sri Vidya' cult of the Shakta tradition. Being highly mystic in 'Svarupa' - primal nature, its grand and subtle 'mantra' is imparted to the initiated only by the Guru. The 'bijaksara' is the 'Panchadashaksari mantra' with fifteen syllabled mantra.

This 'Sahsranama' is a systemised composition of the 'Purvabhaga', 'Nyasa', 'Sahsranama stotra', 'Uttarnyasa' and 'Uttarbhaga' or prologue, placement of the deities, thousand divine names, post placement of the deities and epilogue. The 'Purvabhaga' starts with a humble submission from Agastya to the 'Ashvanana the Lord incarnatae, for the revelation of the manifestation of the Mother-creatrix when she commissioned herself to kill 'Bhandasura'. Sage Agastya was very particular to know the description of 'Sripuram' and the glory of the 'Panchadashakshari mantra'.The sage was also eager to know the mystry of 'Chakraraja vidya' of 'Sri Devi', and other allied system of 'Homa' and 'Homadravya' - Sacrifice and its ingredients.

In this sacred search for 'Truth', 'Sri Hayagriva' cautions the sage to have full devotion and concentration, on his words glorifying the 'Sahsranama'. Certain injunctions were also incorporated by Sri Hayagriva Himself about imparting its sacred knowledge to a 'Shatha' - deceitful, Dusta-cunning and 'Avishvasin' - man without faith. The Sahsranama should be listened to and heard with absolute faith leaving no room for 'Avidya–ignorance'. 'Bhakti' and 'Kirtan' are the two essentials of realising the Highest Truth of the Mother. The 'Japan' – repetition of the sacred mantra and 'Archana' –

recitation of the Names, have been emphasised and authorised. 'Vagdevivasini' were bestowed with Grace to listen to the Glory of Sahsranama, as told by Sri Lalita Herself to them.

The 'Nyasa' starts with 'Vashni-adi-vag devata' as the Rishis of the Lalitasahsranama. The metre is Anushtup, Sri Lalita Tripura-Sundari is the Devata. Aim Srimadvagbhava Kuta is the 'bijam', Klim madhya kuta is the Shakti, Sauh Shaktikuta is the Kilakam. Bijam is seed, Shakti is power and Kilakam is the 'nail' of the Stotram. 'Dhyanam' is of the 'Mula Prakrti' - Primordial nature. 'Nyasa' means to invite and place the Devata in its particular position in the devotees ownself. Devata assumes the 'Mantra' form as the scripture says: 'Mantra in the Deva'. The 'Karanyasa and Anganyasa makes the Devata abide in the hands and the parts of the body. The Devatas abide in the heart, head, skull, eyes and function as 'Kavacham' - the armour of the body and makes all the directions safe leading to 'Bhu, Bhuva and Svah' from the origin, where the devotee and deity are knit together through 'Mantra'.

After meditating upon the glory of Sri Lalita, who is of the form of 'Sindura and Aruna', the formal 'Puja' is followed with the 'gandham, varieties of flowers, dhupam, dipam, amrtmanaivaidhyam and Sarvopcharas'. These are the physical manifestations of the Divine in the form of 'Prithvi - the earthly existence with 'gandha' - colours; 'Akasa' - space with pushpani flowers; 'Vayu' - wind with 'dhupam' or incense, 'Vahni' fire with burning lamp. Amrtam - ambrosia with naivedhyam presents, offering of fruits, cereals and 'Sarvatmika'-integrated elements. These, physical constituents in the worship of Lalita are in the form of mystic phonomes of 'Lam, Ham, Yam, Ram, Vam and Sam'. The meaning and subtle nature of these phonomes are known to the initiated only.

The Sahsranama is a chain of 13 divine episodes in the following manner, comprising the Names and Forms of Sri Lalita :

	Title	Sloka	Name Namavali
1.	Sri Maturvatarah Incarnation of Sri Mata	1 - 21	1 - 54
2.	Sri Nagarvarnana city description	22 - 23	55 - 63
3.	Bhandasurvadhah killing of Bhandasura	24 - 33	64 - 83
4.	Mantrarupah formation of mantra	34 - 35	84 - 87
5.	Kundlinirupah formation of serpent coil	36-40	88 - 111
6.	Bhaktanugrahah compassion over devotees	41 - 42	112 - 125
7.	Nirgunopasana worship of formless	43 - 50	126 - 192
8.	Sagunopasana worship of the manifest	51 - 60	193 - 248
9.	Pancabrahmasvarupah Five fold formation of Brahma	61 - 75	249 - 340
10.	Kshetrakshetrajnarupah formation of kshetraobject, kshetrajna - subject	76 - 81	341 - 372
11.	Pithaniangadevatasea Pittias and angas of Devata	82 - 97	373 - 474
12.	Yogininyasa Placement of Yoginis	98 - 109	475 - 532
13	Vibhutivistara Extension of Vibhutis	110 - 183	533 - 1000

These thirteen episodes represent a journey of Consciousness from Sri Mata to Sri Lalitambika. The Sahsrara of the Supreme Yoga finds its effulgence in these Divine Names. The glory of the Divine Mother is manifest in her Incarnations, description of Sri Nagar, killing of Bhandasura, Mantra form, Kundalini form, Divine grace on the devotees, worship of the 'Absolute, worship of the Manifest, the nature of five fold cosmic principles. The formation of deities with their jurisdiction, the Shakti pithas - seats of Mother Lalita with the host of body guards (Matrkas abiding in the Universal Body); placement of yogini in the micro-macroself, and lastly the complete manifestation and the unification and methodology of the worship.

The Uttarabhaga-epilogue of the Sahsranama throws light on the merits of the recital and worship of Sri Lalita. In the concluding Sloka of the Uttarbhaga Srisuta says that Lord Hayagriva meditated upon Sri Lalitambika, and His heart was filled with Divine Bliss and continued to live in that Supreme ecstasy.

The Sahsranama has been styled in a descriptive and narrative form. The Supreme Effulgence of Sri Lalita is seen in every Name. Her radiance is highly superb. Her Manifestation is the Universal play. She is the Benign Mother who grants the Supreme 'Nivratti' - liberation and 'Pravriti' – the attachment. The scripture says: 'Sadanandapuma vatmaiva paradevata Lalita' one's own self is the source of eternal bliss and Lalita is the Supreme Mother in one's own Atman self.

Acknowledgement

I, the humble devotee of Sri Lalita acknowledge with great reverence the guidance received by me from my father Pandit Niranjan Nath Raina, a traditionalist scholar and Bhakta of Mahatripurasundari-Sri Lalita. Under his instructions the literal translation of Sri Lalitasahsranamavali was undertaken by me. I have included the fascimlo of the first page of Sri Lalitasahsranama written by him in the Sharda script - the ancient script of Kashmir.

I with all humility express that I have been benefitted with the commentary as Sri Lalita Sahsranama published by the Adyar Library and Research Centre, Madras and the Tapavanam series of the Sri Ramakrishna Tapovanam, Tirupparaitturai.

I thank Dr. Satkari Mukhopadhyaya a renowned Sanskrit scholar, the main guiding and illumination force for getting this work published under his care and supervision.

I record the help rendered by Dr. Dev Sharma Vedalankar of Dayanand College, Ajmer, in this work.

Pandit Jagannath Sibu of Kashmir Shakta tradition has given the ritualistic meaning of certain mantras, which I have fairly used.

I also thank M/s. Sharada Publishing House for getting it published.

Chaman Lal Raina

Introduction

Lalita abides in the heart

'Lalita abides in the heart', says Brahma to Markandeya in the Devikavacham! Lalita is the divine Mother, whose heart throbs for the life process. Lalita is the 'Mother of Synthesis' as defined in the Lalitopakhyana an appendage to the Brahmanda Purana. Lalita is Durga, who is worshipped by the Shaktas. She is all emotion, whose sweet face represents the 'Vagbhava' group of mantric syllables. She captures the secret heart-beat of delight, with her Eternal smile. She is the golden sight, who comes down into the heart of the devotees smitting the life with Supreme eternity. The secret name lies in her Eternal attributes which reside in six lotuses in the form of 'Kundalini'. She is not different from the knowledge that brings 'Moksha' - liberation to the bonded soul or 'Jivatman'.

Higher emotion is the primal cause of existence, known as 'Bhavajna'. Being the Supreme energy, she is meditated upon with the loving adoration. Her abode is the Sri Yantra, when adored as Sri Rajrajeshvari. Her feet are the musical metres and the Vedic-Nirukhta is her Lovely face. The Rigveda is her seat. The Yaju and Sam are her thighs. Nyaya and Darshan are the two breasts. The Shruti and Smriti are the lips. The poetics is Her Charming tongue. The Vedanta and other allied subjects are Her eternal eyes, which guides the 'Bhakta' - devotees through intuition, understanding and insight. Her ecstacy is found in 'Gayan, Vadan and Nritya' – song, music and dance.

Lalita is always adored by Ishvara, Sadashiva and a host of Devatas. She is the Mother-Creatrix and the very self of "Satcit-ananda'-truth-consciousness-bliss.

Lalita is the primal source of 'Para, Pashyanti and Madhyama. She is the infinite 'Vaikhari', born from the silence of Eternity. This state of existence is Prakasha and Vimarsha. Her Divine flow is spontaneous. Icha, Kriya and Jnan are Her Manifestatism in the living heart. According to the Shakta school, there is only one

Reality, where Transcendental, Absolute, Immutable, Ineffable Lalita is known as Prakasha - Supreme Effulgence, which contains in itself the seed of consciousness. When it vibrates to manifest of itself, a movement or Icha takes place. This deliberation is known as 'Vimarsha' - reflection. The Kamakala-vilas says that Vimarasha is the reflection of the mirror of Prakasha The Prakasha and Vimarsha are the Shiva and Shakti aspects of Srī Laḷita.

She manifests through the 'Mula trikuna' known as 'Sarvasiddhi-prada chakra' of Lalitambika. The primary triangle is the eternal flame with the 'tejas' of Surya – the solar energy, the 'Soma tattva' – lunar effects and 'Agni' – physical fire. The triadic of 'tejas' are Her three eyes representing the Universal incarnation. She is verily the Vidyavati - the physical, Meta-physical and transcendental knowledge of the triadic mysticism of the Shakti cult. Her charm, glory and silence is seen in the Primal 'Bindu', which is being meditated upon as 'Trikhanda mudra' by the Shodasi worshippers of Sri Lalita. Perception and emotion make Lalita to abide in Sri Chakra where the 'Mula-bindu' is Her heart region. A compassion leans to embrace the physical constituents of 'Jivatman' to make the life cycle a complete one.

Ever gracious Lalita is visualised in the multiple faces of Universal consciousness. Her ways are mysterious, diverse and ever blooming. She is super brilliance, who upholds the mystery of the emotional play. She is fertile and her Emotion is the cosmic union of Kameshvara and Kameshvari. She is Shiva and Shakti, possessed with the singular supreme love. She is the whole, where every part and particle finds its abode in Her. She is self and beyond that, who is meditated upon as the 'Swatantrya Shakti', as visualised by Shiva the Supreme teacher of 'Tandava-nritya' – the cosmic dance. His dance makes the rhythm of Time in its movement, but Lalita transcends the cosmic whirl of Time and is hid in it like a pearl in the sea. She is the Supreme Sovereign, with the authority of 'Chaitanya - consciousness of Being. With her Emotional appearance, she is the fountain head of the nectar of consciousness. Emotion is her primal vibration known as 'Spanda' - which is the source of all creation. She creates and sustains the world with her Love and then makes the world merge in the Higher ego. Filled with compassion, she is fashioned within the heart by Her intellect. Her presence is felt in the heart-cavern. Yogis meditate upon her to realize the infinite digit of immortality. Her song is auspicious with the tune of universal vibration.

The immutable phonomes begin with 'A and end with H'. The great Divine Mother, Lalita is immutable in the form of 'Varnamala' the garland of letters. In this world of name and form, she continues the process of creation through 'Matrikas - the supernal 'Shabda-Brahman'. In the form of languages, she is known as Akshara. Each syllable is potent with her Divine attribute. As Lalita bears and sustains Primal seed in her womb, so all the 'Devas' and 'Matrikas' seed alphabets are the basis of all the 'Mantras' - seed syllables. The seed syllables are occult in nature. The 'Jnanarnava Tantra' states that the sixteen vowels found in the 'Deva Vani' - Sanskrit are a form of Sakti, while the letters beginning with 'क' -ka and ending with 'क्ष' -ksha are the forms of 'Shiva'. The consonents can not be articulated by themselves unless they are in consonance with the vowels. The emotion of Lalita is impregnated with the force of the 'Trayi-vidya', made up of the letters of the three 'Kutas', which are adored with the three 'Hrims' or 'Lajja bija'. Hrim means that the 'Vaikhari' has not come out fully in the open, there is some 'Sankocha' known as a shrinking. 'Hrim bija' is the evolutionary aspect of the Divine.

There are three Hrims in the Mantra, one at the end of each 'Kuta'. The three kutas are triadic in nature and represent the existence of triune - 'Paramatman, Jagat and Jivatman' - God, world and soul. The three kutas are 'Srimadvagbhava kuta, Madhya kuta and Shaktikuta', where Lalita is the presiding deity of the microcosm and macrocosm. Hrim enjoys the identical status of 'Pranava'. Hrim is ethereal existence, illumination and will. It stands for 'Nadabindu', 'Shabda-brahman' or 'Akshara-brahma'. It is the primal digit to evolve into Absolute, and to involve in the number. The adoration of the Hrim leads to the ultimate destiny, where Tripurasundari-Lalita administers the bliss of realization. Hrim is a process of transformation of 'Jiva' into 'Deva' and 'Jiva' into 'jivanmukta'. All the attributes of Lalita are inherent in Hrim. A yogi experiences bliss in terms of 'Ichha, Jnan and Kriya', working under the influence of Lalita, who abides in the 'Ashtasiddhis' of the 'Vasu Kuna' where all the perfections lead to one supreme goal of Lalita's love.

Lalita is all excitement, who lives in the 'Samaya', devoted to the conduct of the 'Samaya chara', who presides over the 'Hum' seed syllable. She embodies the universe in Her golden womb. Her tune is the 'Vina' of Sarasvati, which brings harmony of rhythm and rhyme, power of speech and thought, idea and performance. Conception, Right faith, Right intelligence and Perfection are Her names. She has one thousand attributes, which grants the perfect knowledge of immanence and transcendence. Lalita is beyond 'Varna and Ashrama', yet maintains the law of piety. Her 'Varna' is Supreme love and is easily approached by those, who have the unconditional faith in her Divine play. She is free from name and form, yet endowed with names and forms. She abides in the 'Dashara' - ten spokes of the cosmic wheel of 'Sri-chakra.'

The Eternal knowledge, Allied knowledge are her Names. She is whole-compassion. She is ever charming, grand and utters the eternal sound 'AUM', which grants power to Brahma for creation, Vishnu for preservation and Rudra for annihilation to make the cosmic show a complete one. She is Eternal time, and consumes the serial time in her Lap. She abides in every nerve and cell of Shiva, where she illumines the spirit of Shiva by accepting Him as Her very Self. She is the embodiment of Yakini, Hakini, Dakini, Rakini, Lakini, Kakini and Sakini Devis. Love, Emotion, excitement are her psychic energies.

She transcends action and inaction. She shines among the 'Kula' system and is worshipped through the 'Kadi' mantra, the first letter of this seed-syllable of the Pancadasi mantra. Her expansion is vast, who maintains the harmony of the 'Triadic mysticism' of 'Shiva-Shakti-anu' and 'Mahakali, Mahalakshmi, Mahasarasvati'. Being the compassionate Mother, she bestows, grace to the 'Matrikas' - little mothers. Being Gayatri, as Mother of Vedas, she holds all scriptures in her Lap. Great substance is found in Her. She is the Cosmic breath of yoga and Her manifestation is seen in the fourteen triangles of Sri-Yantra.

Her Eternal love is filled with her Eternal grace, which is without beginning or end. She is all beauty found in the Primal figure. Her seat is the primal triangle of Sri Yantra, and is revered with 'Yoni mudra'. She manifests for the work of 'Devas', born from the alter of the fire of consciousness. Her supramental consciousness is to save the world from 'Avidya' - ignorance. As saviour of the 'Devas' - divine forces, she assumes the characteristics of Para shakti, where She makes the cosmic energies to concentrate in one unified energy. She assumes the form of 'Mahalakshmi' - Adya-shakti, and the 'Devas' adore her Feet with 'Lakhsarasa', and thus make the triple world - 'Bhu, Bhuva, Svaha' dance to her Tune. She takes 'Hari and Hara' in her lap to help in maintaining the balance between emotion and intellect. She is the Supreme intuition, who abides in the sixteen petalled lotus of Sri-chakra.

She is the embodiment of 'Panchadashakshri and Shodasi' mantra and of 'Hadi vidya and Kadi vidya'. She is occult yet seen with devotion and from the original Throb which in its subtle form is Light. Her each mystic syllable evolves, with the rise of the moon in the 'Shukla paksha' - lunar fortnight and is meditated upon on the 'Purnima' as the Moon is just a cosmic beauty of her Appearance. She is Universal seer, who imparts the sacred knowledge of 'Tripura Sundari' mantra to reconstitute the perfect word or 'Akshara'. She therefore, resides in the Shodasi mantra. Her grace is a flow and her face is deeply aglow with ambrosia. To bestow prosperity is one of her Functions and as Vaishnavi she abides in Vibhava - wealth and final beautitude, closely related to Aksharabrahma.

Lalita is the Supreme authority and discharges her Eternal function through Brahmi, Vaishnavi and Raudri Shakti. She abides in the form of 'Sahsrara' - the thousand spokes of the mystic lotus. She is material existence of 'Navadvipas' – nine continents and Saptasindhus – seven oceans. She is the source light of the sun and her Radiance is far exalted. The brilliance of thousand of solar galaxies can not excel her Triadic beauty.

Being 'Vagdevi', she is adored as 'Varnamayi Ambika'. She is the 'Mantra' and not different from it. This 'Rahasya' - secret knowledge is known as 'Tripura Sundari Karuna' - the compassion of the Mother. Peace, Force, Light and Delight are constantly experienced in Her 'Mantra'. The secret of great achievement is revealed only through the Grace of Lalita. Lalita is a source of inspiration and transformation.

Auspiciousness, Beauty and Emotion are her Female characteristics being appreciated in the 'Agamas'. She is also triple-footed with Triple knowledge and Triple image, who resides in the 'Tripura' – the city of triple image. She envelops the whole creation in the 'Muladhara' triange, which is the affirmation of the essential spirit. 'Tripura-Sundari' is the spirit of 'Purna Yoga'. The three circles of Sri Chakra are the forms of mind, over-mind and supermind. Being 'Anadi' - beginingless in 'Svarupa' - primal form, there is no end to Her atrributes, yet She abides in the Sri Yantra.

A nine-fold classification is adopted to comprehend the symbology of the Sri Yantra, where 'Tripura, Tripureshi, Tripurasundari, Tripuravasini, Tripurashri, Tripuramalini, Tripurasiddha, Tripurambika and Mahatripurasundari' are adored as the nine Presiding Devis. Lalita is one is all and All is one.

To bow to Sri Lalita, who abides in the heart region, is the keen desire of the devotees, who feel Her presence in every pulsation of life. She is splendidly graceful and incites primordial nature and transmigratory jivas at the beginning of every new cycle of creation.

ॐ

AUM

श्रीललिताम्बिकासहस्रनामस्तोत्रम्

Sri Lalitam Ambika Sahasranama Stotra

अगस्त्य उवाच

Agastya said

1. अश्वानन महाबुद्धे सर्वशास्त्रविशारद ।
कथितं ललितादेव्याश्चरितं परमादभुतम् ।।

O very wise and highly proficient one in all the scriptures Ashvanama! you have told me the divine chritam – life aspect of Sri Lalita Devi.

2. पूर्वं प्रदुर्मवा मानुस्ततः पट्टाभिषेचनम् ।
भण्डासुरवधश्चैव विस्तरेण त्वयोदितः ।।

You have narrated the manifestration of the Divine Mother Lalita, followed by Her coronation and slaining of Bhandasura in detail.

3. वर्णित श्रीपुरञ्चापि महाविमवविस्तरम् ।
श्रीमत्पञ्चदशाक्षर्या महिमा वर्णितस्तथा ।।

You have also narrated the grandeur and splendeur of Sripuram and the supreme efficiency of Srimat-Panchadasha akshara – fifteen-syllabled mantra of 'Sri Vidya'.

4. षोढान्यासादयो न्यासाः न्यासखण्डे समीरिताः ।
अन्तयगि क्रमश्चैव बहियोग क्रमस्तथा ।।

Also you have explained the Shodhanyasa – Six placements and the nyasakhanda – subdivisions of placements, followed by 'antarayaga miners and bahirayaga krama' – the inner and outer sequences of workship and meditation.

5. महायागक्रमश्चापि पूजाखण्डे प्रकीर्तितः ।
परश्चरणखण्डे त जपलक्षणमीरितम् ।।

Verily, you explained the 'mahayaga krama' – sequence of great and supreme yaga in the puja-khanda' – mode of worship and threw light on the symptomatie japam in the 'purushacharan khandam'

6. होमखण्डे त्वया प्रोक्तो होमद्रव्यविधिक्रमः।
चक्रराजस्य विद्यायाः श्रीदेव्याः देशिकात्मनोः।।

You explained the ingredients essentially required in this mode of worship in the 'homakhanda' – sacrificial part and also the knowledge of Chakraraja, which is the integral abode of Sri Devi.

7. रहस्यखण्डे तादात्म्य परस्परमुदीरितम्।
स्तोत्रखण्डे बहुविद्याः स्तुतयः मरिकीर्तिताः।।

You also threw light on the identity aspect in the 'rahasya-khanda' – the mystic portion and the 'stotra-khanda' – the devotional portion, which is a synthesis of different 'stutis' – devotional songs exalting the Divine Mother.

8. मन्त्रिणीदण्डिनीदेव्योः प्रोक्ते नाम सहस्त्रके।
न तु श्रीललितादेव्याः प्रोक्तं नामसहस्त्रकम्।।

During the discourse of Sahasranama, you have mentioned the names of Mantrini and Dandini Devis, but nothing has been told about the Sahsnnama – the thousand attributes of Sri Lalita Devi.

9. तत्र मे संशयो जातो हयग्रीव दयानिधे।
किं वा त्वया विस्मृतं तद् तान्वा वा समुपेक्षितम्।।

You are the treasure house of compassion, O Hayagriva! But you have deliberately kept me ignorant about it, or you have forgotten to tell me about the Sahsranama of Sri Lalita. So the doubt has crept in my mind.

10. मम वा योग्यता नास्ति श्रोतुं नामसहस्त्रकम्।
किमर्थं भवता नोक्तं तत्र मे कारणं वद।।

Do I not possess the faculty of listening to the Sahsranama? O revered master! Why did you not reveal to me the same Sahasanama?

सूत उवाच

Suta said:

11. इति पृष्टो हयग्रीवो मुनिना कुम्भजन्मना।
प्रहृष्टो वचनं प्राह तापसं कुम्भसम्भवम्।।

Having been asked the same by the 'pot-born' Muni, Hayagriva, thus he told the following words to the 'Tapasavi Kumbha-sambhava' – born out of pot.

श्रीहयग्रीव उवाच

Sri Hayagriva said:

12. लोपामुद्रापतेऽगस्त्य सावधानमनाः शृणु।
नाम्नां सहस्र यन्नोक्त कारणं तद् वदामि ते।।

O Agastya, the spouse of Lopamudra! Listen to me with careful mind! I will let you know the reason why I did not reveal to you the mind Sahasranama.

13. रहस्यमिति मत्वाहं नोक्तवांस्ते न चान्यथा।
पुनश्च पृच्छसे भक्त्या तस्मात् तत् ते वदाम्यहम्।।

As Sahsranama is highly occult, so I did not reveal the same to you. No other reason forbade me to reveal the same to you. Since you seem to be very eager devotee, I reveal the same to you.

14. ब्रूयाच्छिष्याय भक्ताय रहस्यमपि देशिकः।
भवता न प्रदेय स्यादभक्ताय कदाचन।।

Knowledge of the Deshika should only be revealed to a disciple who is the genuine devotee. It should never be imparted, who is not a sincere devotee

15. न शठाय न दुषाय नाविश्वासाय कर्हिचत्
श्रीमातृमक्तियुक्ताय श्रीविद्याराजेदिने।।

The secrets of Sri Vidya should only be revealed to those, who have faith and devotion in Sri Mata, and not to those who happen to be cheat, inhumane, without trust and belief.

16. उपासकाय शुद्धाय देयं नामसहस्रकम्।
यानि नामसहस्राणि सद्यः सिद्धिप्रदानि वै।।

The thousand names should be given to the upasaka with pure heart, as there thousand attributes give all perfection in every sphere of life.

17. तन्त्रेषु ललितादेव्यास्तेषु मुख्यमिदं मुने।
श्रीविद्यैव तु मन्त्राणां तत्र कादिर्यथा परा।।

O Muni! Lalita Devi is the Supreme among all the tantras and Sri Vidya excells in all the Mantras and there in also Kadi Mantra is supremely transcendental.

18. पुराणां श्रीपुरमिव शक्तीनां ललिता यथा।
श्रीविद्योपासकाना च यथा देवो वरः शिवः।।

Sripuram is the holiest of all the puras (cities) and Sri Lalita is supreme among all the Shaktis. For the Upasakas of Sri Vidya Shiva alone is the Supreme Deva.

19. तथा नामसहस्रेषु वरमेतत् प्रकीर्तितम्।
यथास्य पठनाद् देवी प्रीयते ललिताम्बिका।।

Of all the Sahasranamas, this alone is the Supreme superb and excellent. Who so ever recites this Sahsrenama, happens to be very dear to Sri Lalita Ambika.

20. अन्यनाम सह स्रस्य पाठान्न प्रीयते तथा।
श्रीमानुः प्रीतये तस्मादनिशं कीर्तयेदिदम्।।

She does not get so much pleased with the reitation of other Sahsranamas. It should be recited throughout as the Mother-Creatrise isvery fond of it.

21. बिल्व पत्रैश्चक्रराजे योऽर्चयेल्ललिताम्बिकाम्।
पद्मैर्वा तुलसीपत्रैरेभिनमिसहस्रकैः।।

Whose ever worship Lalita-Ambika in the form of Sri Yantra lotus, tulsileaves, reciting this Sahsranama, then....,

22. सद्यः प्रसादं कुरुते तस्य सिंहासनेश्वरी।
चक्राधिराजमभ्यर्च्य जप्त्वा पञ्चदशाक्षरीम्।।

The Mother-Creatrix on the couch of a lion bestows grace upon him. After worshipping the Supreme Chakraraja properly, the Japan of Panchadeshakshari should be performed.

23. जपान्ते कीर्तयेन्निन्यमिदं नामसहस्त्रकम् ।
जप पूजाद्यशक्तोऽपि पठेनमसहस्त्रकम् ।।

After 'Japani', this Sahsranama should be recited in Kirtana always. Whosoever may be inable to do Japan, puja, etc., still should read this sacred Salisranama.

24. साङ्गार्चने साङ्गजपे यन् फलं तदवाप्नुयात् ।
उपासने स्तुतीरन्याः पठेदम्युदयो हि सः ।।

The Upasana stuti, archana with all its limbs and japan with all its limbs of other deities give prosperly to the devotee, but merely reciting of this Sahsrenama grants all grace and prosperity.

25. इदं नामसहस्रं तु कीर्तयेन्निन्यकर्मवत् ।
चक्रराजार्चनं देव्या जपो नाम्ना च कीर्तनमू ।।

Kirtanam of this Sahasranama should be performed in the manner of 'nitya-karma' – eternal duty & along with the archana of Chakraraja and japan of the thousand names of Sri Lalita.

26. भक्तस्य कृत्यमेतावद् अन्यदम्युदयं विदुः ।
भक्तस्यावश्यकम्रिदं नामसाहस्त्रकीर्मनम् ।।

The devotee is required to do essentially the recital of this Sahsranama , it would lead him to every sort of prosperity.

27. तत्र हेतुं प्रवक्ष्यामि शृणु त्वं कुम्भसम्भव ।
पुरा श्रीललितादेवी भक्तानां हितकाम्यया ।।

O sage Agastya, Kumbha - born! I am narrating to you the prospectus of the favour granted to the devotees by Sri Lalita Devi. So you listen to it.

वाग्देवीवशिनी मुख्याः समाहूयेदमब्रवीत् ।

Thus invited Vagdevi-Vashini host of chief devis and said.

श्रीललितिम्बिका उबावः

Sri Lalitambika said

28. वाग्देवता वशिन्याद्याः शृणुध्वं वचनं मम ।।

O Devis,Vagdevi Vashini etc., you listen to my words.

29. भवत्यो मत्प्रसादेन प्रोल्लसद्वाग्विभूतयः ।
मद्भक्तानां वाग्विमूतिप्रदाने विनियोजिताः ।।

You are engrossed with all the vibhutis, hence I commission you all to grant 'Vag-Vibhutis the power of speech and exalted attributes to my dear devotees.

30. मच्चक्रस्य रहस्यज्ञा मम नामपरायणाः ।
मम स्तोत्रविधानाय तस्मादाज्ञापयामि वः ।।

I command you to impart their divine knowledge of my stotra-vidhana methodology of adoration, as you are fully conscious of the mysteries of my chakra and the efficacy of 'Name and form'.

31. कुरुध्वमङ्कितं स्तोत्रं मम नामसहस्रकैः ।
येन भक्तैः स्तुताया मे सद्यः प्रीतिः परा भवेत् ।।

You compose a stotra of my thousand names; with which the devotees are able to adore me with 'Bhakti' (devotion) so that they may become very dear and near to me.

श्रीहयग्रीव उवाचः

Sri Hayagriva said

32. इत्याज्ञप्रा वचो देव्यः श्रीदेव्या ललिताम्नया ।
रहस्यैर्नामभिर्दिण्यैश्चक्रुः स्तोत्रमनुत्तमम् ।।

Having thus commanded by Sri Devi Lalitambika, the Vag Devis composed the mystic 'Nama-stotram', after having realized this unparalleled divine laudation.

33. रहस्यनामसाहस्रमिति तद् विश्रुत परम् ।
ततः कदाचित् सदसि स्थित्वा सिंहासनेऽम्बिका ।।

After it composition, mother Lalitambika who was on the couch of a lion, heard this highly occult Sahsranama after some durations, while sitting in her sanctum sanctorum.

34. स्वसेवावसरं प्रादान् सर्वेषां कुम्भसम्भव ।
सेवार्थमागतास्तत्र ब्रहनाणीब्रह्मकोटयः ।।

O pot-born Muni! Millions of millions Brahmas and Brahmanis gathered there to submit before the Mother-Creatix to get a chance to serve in her presence, along with other.

35. लक्ष्मीनारायणानां च कोटयः समुपागताः।
गौरीकोटिसमेतानां रुद्राणामपि कोटयः।।

Millions of Lakshmi & Narayanas also reached along with Gauris and Rudras in the multitude of million of numbers.

36. मन्त्रिणीदण्डिनीमुख्याः सेवार्थं या समागताः।
शक्तयो विविधाकारास्तासां संख्या न विद्यते।।

Besides, chief of Mantrinis and Dandinis also came for the purposes of Serving the Mother, Lalita. All other Shaktis with vanjing formation can not be enumerated, who presented themselves before the mother.

37. दिव्यौधा मानवौधाश्च सिद्धौधाश्च समागताः।
तत्र श्रीललितादेवी सर्वेषां दर्शनं ददौ।।

The multitude of 'brilliant ones', 'human-beings', and 'perfect ones' gathered there, before Sri Lalita Devi and the Devi graced all of them with her 'Darshanam' appearance.

38. तेषु दृष्ट्वोपविष्टेशु स्वे स्वे स्थाने यथाक्रमम्।
तत्र श्रीललितादेवी कटाक्षक्षेपणोदिताः।।

Sri Lalita Devi saw them seated in their respective places observed them with side-glanced twist and accordingly commanded.

39. उत्थाय वशिनीमुख्या बद्धाञ्जलिपुटास्तदा।
अस्तुवन्नामसाहस्रैः स्वकृतैर्ललिताम्बिकाम्।।

Vashini and lost of other prominent Devis joined their palms together, adored Lalitambika with the Sahasranama, composed by themselves in praise of the Mother-Creatrix.

40. श्रुत्वा स्तवं प्रसन्नाभूल्ललिता परमेश्वरी।
ते सर्वे विस्मयं जग्मुर्ये तत्र सदसि स्थिताः।।

On hearing their obeisance, Supreme Sovereign Mother Lalita got pleased with them. All of them got wandered, who were present in that assembly.

41. ततो प्रोवाच ललिता सदस्यान् देवतागणान्।

Thereafter Lalita Devi pronounced to the assembled host of Devatas-brilliant ones.

श्रीललिताम्बिका उवाच

Sri Lalitambika said

41. ममाज्ञयैव वाग्देव्यश्चक्रुः स्तोत्रमनुत्तमम् ।।

Under the authority of my own being, vagdevis have composed this supreme stotram.

42. अङ्कितं नाममिर्दिव्यैर्मम प्रीतिविधायकैः ।
तत पठध्वं सदा यूयं स्तोत्रं मत्प्रीतिवृद्धये ।।

All of you, always do recite the divine attributer of mine properly drafted, for my Satisfaction. It will enhance the higher satisfaction and joy.

43. प्रवर्तयध्वं भक्तेषु मम नामसहस्रकम् ।
इदं नामसहस्रं मे यो भक्तः पठते सकृतृ ।।

Do popularize this Sahasranama among my devotees. Who so ever be the devotee of mine reading constantly this Sahasranama..,

44. स मे प्रियतमो ज्ञेयस्तस्मै कामान् ददाम्यहम् ।
श्रीचक्रे मां समभ्यर्च्य जप्त्वा पञ्चदशाक्षरीम् ।।

He becomes very dear to me and I fulfil all her desires, when he adores me in the image of Srichara after doing japan of Panchadashakshari - fifteen - syllabled mantra.

45. पश्चान्नामसहस्रं मे कीर्तयेन्मम तुष्टये ।
मामर्चयतु वा मा वा विद्यां जपतु ।।

Afterwards for my contentment, the 'Kirtanam' of thousand names should be recited. The devotee may do 'archana' - laudation and perform 'japam' of Sri Vidya.

46. कीर्तयेन्नामसाहस्रमिदं मत्प्रीतये सदा ।
मत्प्रीत्या सकलान्कामान् लभते नात्र संशयः ।।

The 'Kirtanam' of this Sahasranama should be performed solely for my pleasure. 'After I get pleased, the devotee achieves duly all his desires fulfilled, there is no doubt about it.

तस्मान्नामसहस्रं मे कीर्तयध्वं सदाऽऽदरात् ।

Hence do recite the 'kirtanam' of my Sahasranama, with great reverence constantly.

श्रीहयग्रीव उवाच

Sri Hayagriva Said

47. इति श्रीललितेशानी शास्ति देवान् सहानुमान् ।

Thus Supreme Sovereign Sri Lalita Devi commands with the host of Devis to the Devas.

48. तदाज्ञया तदारम्य ब्रहमविष्णुमहेश्वराः ।
शक्तयो मन्त्रिणीमुख्या इदं नाम सहस्रकम् ।।

Since then, under her instructions Brahama, Vishnu, Maheshvara, Mantrini and prominent Shaktis do recite this Sahasranama.

49. पठन्ति भक्त्य सततं ललितापरितुष्टये ।
तस्मादवश्यं भक्तेन कीर्तनीयमिदं मुने ।।

For all the contentment of Lalita Devi all the devotees recite this Stotram. Therefore, O Muni Agastya! You should with all promptness and devotion recite its Kirtanam.

50. आवश्यकत्वे हेतुस्ते मया प्रोक्तो मुनीश्वर ।
इदानीं नामसाहस्र वष्यामि श्रद्धया श्रृणु ।।

O sage among Munis! I am conveyed you the essentials of this episode. You listen to this Sahasranama with great devotion, which I am narrating to you.

इति श्रीब्रह्माण्डपुराणे उत्तरखण्डे श्रीहयग्रीवागस्त्य -
संवादे श्रीललिताम्बिकासहस्रनामस्तोत्रस्य पूर्वभागः

Here ends the prologue of the thousand names of Sri Lalitambika during the discourse between Sri Hayagriva and Agastya incorporated in the Uttarkhanda of Sri Brahmanda - purana.

अथ न्यासादि-विधि

The Methodology of Nyasas – placement

आचमनम्-श्रीं ह्रीं क्लीं ऐं सौः

Achamanam (Sipping of fresh water) reciting the mantra Shrim - Hrim - Klim - Aim - Sauh.

मूलमन्त्रः— पञ्चादशाक्षरी

Mulamantra - (Primal mantras) is Panchadashaksham (to be learnt under the initiation of a celebrated Guru of the Lalita tradition)

अस्य श्रीललिताम्बिकासहस्रनामस्तोत्रमालामहामन्त्रस्य वशिन्यादिवाग्देवता ऋषयः। अनुष्टुप् छन्दः। श्रीललिताम्बिका परमेश्वरी देवता। श्रीमद्वाग्भवकूटेति बीजम्। मध्यकूटेति शक्तिः। शक्तिकूटेति कीलकम्। मूलप्रकृतिरिति ध्यानम्। श्रीललितामहात्रिपुर सुन्दरी प्रसाद सिद्धि द्वारा चिन्तित फलावाप्त्यर्थे जपे विनियोगः।

The Vashinyadi Vagdevta are the Rishis of this Sri Lalitambika - Sahsranama - Stotra - mala - maha - mantra. Anushtupa is the metre. Sri Lalitambika Parmeshvari is the Devata. Srimadvagbhava Kuta is the bijam - seed. Madhyakuta is the Shakti - power. Shakti Kuta is the Kilkan - nailing. Madhya Kuta prakriti is the dhyanam - meditation. The Viniyoga - pronouncement of doing the japam - repitition of name is the achievement of desired frunt of my choice. in submission for the perfection of this patham is obeisance to Sri Lalita Maha Tripura Sundari, through her benign grace.

ऋष्यादिन्यासः

Presence of Divinity in Rishis

वशिन्यादिभ्यो वाग्देवताभ्यः ऋषिभ्यो नमः (शिरसि)

I bow to Vashinyedi Vagdevata Rishis, who abide in my head.

अनुष्टुप्छन्दसे नमः (मुखे)

I bow to Anushtup metre, which abides in the month.

श्रीमहात्रिपुरसुन्दर्यै देवतायै नमः (हृदये)

I bow to Sri Mahatripura Sundari Devata who abides in the heart.

कबीजाय नमः नाभौ

I bow to 'Ka' seed, which is in the navel.

सशक्तये नमः (गुहये)

I bow to 'Sa' Shakti - power, which is hidden in the anus.

हकीलकाय नमः (पादयोः)

I bow to 'Ha', which is nailing in the feel.

चतुर्विधपुरुषार्थसिध्यर्थे जपे विनियोगः (सर्वाङ्गे)

I feel the presence in my whole body for the fourfoldPurushartha of Dharma - Artha - Kama - Moksha, for which I take vow for japam.

श्रीललितामट्टारिकामहात्रिपुरसुन्दरी देवता।

Sri Lalita Bhattarika Mahatripura-Sundari is the Devata.

ऐं बीजम। सौः शक्ति। क्लीं कीलकम्। मम चतुर्विधपुरुषार्थसिध्यर्थे जपे विनियोगः।

Seed is Aim; power is Sauh; nailing is Klim, I do viniyoga of japam for my four fold Purusharthas.

करन्यासः
Presence of Divinity in hands

ऐं अङ्गुष्ठाभ्यां नमः। क्लीं तर्जनीभ्यां नमः। सौः मध्यमाभ्यां नमः।
सौः अनामिकाभ्यां नमः।
क्लीं कनिष्ठिकाभ्यां नमः। ऐं करतलकरपृष्ठाभ्यां नमः।

I bow to Aim, which rests in the thumbs. I bow to Klim, which rests in the first fingers. I bow to Sauh, which rests in the mid fingers. I bow to Sauh, which rests in the ring fingers. I bow to Klim, which rests in the small fingers. I bow to Aim which rests in the palm and reversed palm.

अथाङ्गन्यासः
Presence of divinity in limbs

ऐं हृदयाय नमः । क्लीं शिरसे स्वाहा । सौः शिखायै वष्ट । सौ कवचाय हुं । क्लीं नेत्राय वौषट् । ऐं अस्त्राय फट् भूर्भुवः सुवरोमिति दिग्बन्धः ।

I bow to Aim, which is the heart, to Klim which is head, to Sauh which is the tuft i.e. Vashat. To sauh hum which is armour, to klim vashat which are eyes. Aim phat for arms. I build the direction, which is manifestation of Bhu, Bhuva and Svah.

ध्यानम्
Dhyanam

सिन्दूरारुणविग्रहां त्रिणयनां माणिक्यमौलिस्फुरम्–
तारानायकशेखरां स्मितमुखीमापीनवक्षोरुहाम् ।
पाणिम्यामलिपूर्णरत्नचषकं रक्तोत्पलं बिभ्रतीं
सौम्यां रत्नघटस्थरक्तचरणां ध्यायेत्परामम्बिकाम् ।।

I bow and surrender to her feet and take refuge in her, who is of triple eyes. Her hue is that of red 'Sindura's wearing the diadem of precious stones and a crescent is shining wonderfully on it. She is easily accessible with her benign smile. Her children get an inexhaustible store of 'life-milk' in her full breasts. She has vessel of honey in one hand and the red lotus in the other. It symbolises joy and wisdom. She has placed her feet on the precious pot full of valuable gems indicating that she is easily attainable.

अरुणां करुणातरङ्गिताक्षीं धृतपाशाङ्गताक्षीं धृतपाशाङ्कुशपुष्पबाणचापाम् ।
अणिमादिभिरावृतां मयूरवैरहमित्येव विभावये भवानीम् ।।

I bow make obeisance to the Mother - Creatrix Bhavani with the radiance I do posses, with her benign glance of her compassionate waves of the dawn, ever present and vibrant in her eyes. It is she who possesses moose, goad, flower, 'bow and arrow' in her hands. She is always surrounded by Anima etc. as the siddhis with eight perfections.

ध्यायेत् पद्मासनस्थां विकसितवदनां पद्मपत्रायताक्षीं
हेमाभां पीतवस्त्रां करकलितलसद्धेमपद्मां वराङ्गीम्।
सर्वालङ्कारयुक्तां सततमभयदां भक्तनम्रां भवानीं
श्रीविद्यां शान्तमूर्तिं सकलसुरनुतां सर्वसम्पत्प्रदात्रीम्।।

Let me meditate upon 'Sri Vidya', 'Shantamurti' the manifestation of eternal peace, who is ever bowed by all the Devas. She is seated on the couch of lotus. Her face is ever smiling and is looking grand with the eyes resembling lotus leaves. Her hue is that of gold, wearing the yellow garments. She keeps the golden lotus in her hand and her being is ever radiant. She is ornamented with all the jewellery, and is the embodiment with all the jewellery, and is the embodiment of 'Adhaya' – forgiveness who bow at her feet. She alone grants all the prosperity to the devotees, who surrender at her feet.

सकुङ्कुमविलेपनामलिकचुम्बिकस्तूरिकां
समन्दहसितेक्षणां सशरचापपाशाकुशाम्।
अशेषजनमोहिनीमरुणमाल्यभूषाम्बरां
जपाकुसुमभासुरां जपविधौ स्मरेदम्बिकाम्।।

Let me remember Ambika at the time of Japam, who is annointed with the gentle touches of 'Kumkum', and 'Kasturi'. Her benign eyes are filled with the amusement, and is holding noose, goad bow and arrow in her hands. She enchants all the creatures while puts on the ornament of dawn like garland and garments like of Japakusum lisbiscus flowers.

लमित्यादिपञ्चपूजा

Fine fold puja of Lam etc.

लं पृथ्वीतत्त्वात्मिकायै श्रीललिताम्बिकायै गन्धं परिकल्पयामि।

I offer gandham - sandal etc. to Sri Lalitambika, with the form of 'Lam', which is the manifestation of Prithvi-tattva ' earthly element.

हं आकाशतत्त्वात्मिकायै श्रीललिताम्बिकायै पुष्पं परिकल्पयामि।

I offer flower to Sri Lalitambika, with the form of 'Ham', which is the manifestation of Akaska-tattva earthly element.

यं वायुतत्त्वात्मिकायै श्रीललिताम्बिकायै धूपं परिकल्पयामि ।

I offer 'dhupam' to Sri Lalitambika. with the form of Vam, which is the manifestation of 'Vayu-tattva' air element.

रंवहितत्त्वात्मिकायै श्रीलालताम्बिकायै दीपं परिकल्पयामि ।

I offer 'Dipam' lamp/light to Sri Lalitambika, with the form of 'Ram', which is the manifestation of 'Vahni-tatva' - fine element.

वं अमृततत्त्वात्मिकायै श्रीललिताम्भिकायै अमृतं नैवेद्यं परिकल्पयामि ।

I offer 'Amritan nairedyam' ambrosia and presentation to Sri lalitambika, with the form of 'Van', which is the manifestation 'Amrita-tattva' - ambrosial element.

सं सर्वतत्त्वात्मिकायै श्रीललिताम्बिकायै ताम्बूल सर्वोपचारान् परिकल्पयामि ।

I offer 'Tambul and Sarva upchara' - fruits and all the varieties of Sugar, Liney etc. to Sri Lalitambika with the form of 'Sam', which is the manifestation of 'Sarva-tattva'– all the element.

इति स्तोत्रादौ ऋष्यादिन्यास पञ्च पूजान्तं कृत्वा सहस्रनामस्तोत्रपाराणानन्तरं श्रीदेव्या दक्षिणहस्ते जल धारा पूर्वकं तत्समर्पणं कुर्यात् ।

After performing the 'Rishi-adi-nyasa', pancha-puja, the recitation of Sahsranama-stotram should be done and submitted it to Sri Devi Water should be poured in the right have with samarpanam full surrender with devotion

ललितासहस्रनामस्तोत्रम्

श्रीमाता श्रीमहाराज्ञी श्रीमत्सिंहासनेश्वरी।
चिदग्निकुण्डसंभूता देवकार्यसमुद्यता।। १ ।।

उद्यद्भानुसहस्राभा चतुर्बाहुसमन्विता।
रागस्वरूपपाशाढ्या क्रोधाकाराङ्कुशोज्ज्वला।। २ ।।

मनोरूपेक्षुकोदण्डा पञ्चतन्मात्रसायका।
निजारूणप्रभापूरमज्जद्ब्रह्माण्डमण्डला।। ३ ।।

चम्पकाशोकपुन्नागसौगन्धिकलसत्कचा।
कुरुविन्दमणिश्रेणीकनत्कोटीरमण्डिता।। ४।।

अष्टमीचन्द्रविभ्राजदलिकस्थलशोभिता।
मुखचन्द्रकलङ्काभमृगनाभिविशेषका।। ५।।

वदनस्मरमाङ्गल्यगृहतोरणचिल्लिका।
वक्त्रलक्ष्मीपरीवाहचलन्मीनाभलोचना।। ६ ।।

नवचम्पकपुष्पाभनासादण्डविराजिता।
ताराकान्तितिरस्कारिनासाभरणभासुरा।। ७ ।।

कदम्बमञ्जरीक्लृप्तकर्णपुरमनोहरा।
ताटङ्कयुगलीभूततपनोडुपमण्डला।। ८ ।।

पद्मरागशिलादर्शपरिभाविकपोलभूः।
नवविद्रुमबिम्बश्रीन्यक्कारिरदनच्छदा।। ९ ।।

शुद्धविद्याङ्कुराकारद्विजपङ्क्तिद्वयोज्ज्वला।
कर्पूरवीटिकामोदसमाकर्षद्दिगन्तरां।। १० ।।

निजसंलापमाधुर्यविनिर्भर्त्सितकच्छपी।
मन्दस्मितप्रभापूरमज्जत्कामेशमानसा।। ११ ।।

अनाकलितसादृश्यचिबुकश्रीविराजिता।
कामेशबद्धमाङ्गल्यसूत्रशोभितकंधरा।। १२ ।।

कनकाङ्गदकेयूरकमनीयभुजान्विता।
रत्नग्रैवेयचिन्ताकलोलमुक्ताफलान्विता।। १३ ।।

कामेश्वरप्रेमरत्नमणिप्रतिपणस्तनी।
नाभ्यालवालरोमालिलताफलकुचद्वयी।। १४ ।।

लक्ष्यरोमलताधारतासमुन्नेयमध्यमा।
स्तनभारदलन्मध्यपट्टबन्धवलित्रया।। १५ ।।

अरुणारुणकौसुम्भवस्त्रभास्वत्कटीतटी।
रत्नकिङ्किणिकारम्यरशनादामभूषिता।। १६ ।।

कामेशज्ञातसौभाग्यमार्दवोरुद्वयान्विता।
माणिक्यमकुटाकारजानुद्वयविराजिता।। १७ ।।

इन्द्रगोपपरिक्षिप्तस्मरतूणाभजङ्घिका।
गूढगुल्फा कूर्मपृष्ठजयिष्णुप्रपदान्विता।। १८ ।।

नखदीधितिसंछन्ननमज्जनतमोगुणा।
पदद्वयप्रभाजालपराकृतसरोरुहा।। १९ ।।

शिञ्जानमणिमञ्जीरमण्डितश्रीपदाम्बुजा।
मरालीमन्दगमना महालावण्यशेवधिः।। २० ।।

सर्वारुणाऽनवद्याङ्गी सर्वाभरणभूषिता।
शिवकामेश्वराङ्कस्था शिवा स्वाधीनवल्लभा।। २१ ।।

सुमेरुमध्यशृङ्गस्था श्रीमन्नगरनायिका।
चिन्तामणिगृहान्तःस्था पञ्चब्रह्मासनस्थिता।। २२ ।।

महापद्माटवीसंस्था कदम्बवनवासिनी।
सुधासागरमध्यस्था कामाक्षी कामदायिनी।। २३ ।।

देवर्षिगणसंघातस्तूयमानात्मवैभवा।
भण्डासुरवधोद्युक्तशक्तिसेनासमन्विता।। २४ ।।

संपत्करीसमारूढसिंधुरव्रजसेविता।
अश्वारूढाधिष्ठिताश्वकोटिकोटिभिरावृता।। २५ ।।

चक्रराजरथारूढसर्वायुधपरिष्कृता।
गेयचक्ररथारूढमन्त्रिणीपरिसेविता ।। २६ ।।

किरिचक्ररथारूढदण्डनाथपुरस्कृता।
ज्वालामालिनिकाक्षिप्तवह्निप्राकारमध्यगा।। २७ ।।

भण्डसैन्यवधोद्युक्तशक्तिविक्रमहर्षिता।
नित्यापराक्रमाटोपनिरीक्षणसमुत्सुका।। २८ ।।

भण्डपुत्रवधोद्युक्तबालाविक्रमनन्दिता।
मन्त्रिण्यम्बाविरचितविषङ्गवधतोषिता।। २९ ।।

विशुक्रप्राणहरणवाराहीवीर्यनन्दिता।
कामेश्वरमुखालोककल्पितश्रीगणेश्वरा।। ३० ।।

महागणेशनिर्भिन्नविघ्नायन्त्रप्रहर्षिता।
भण्डासुरेन्द्रनिर्मुक्तशस्त्रप्रत्यस्त्रवर्षिणी।। ३१ ।।

कराङ्गुलिनखोत्पन्ननारायणदशाकृतिः।
महापाशुपतास्त्राग्निनिर्दग्धासुरसैनिका।। ३२ ।।

कामेश्वरास्त्रनिर्दग्धसभण्डासुरसैनिका (शून्यका)।
ब्रह्मोपेन्द्रमहेन्द्रादिदेवसंस्तुतवैभवा।। ३३ ।।

हरनेत्राग्निसंदग्धकामसंजीवनौषधिः।
श्रीमद्वाग्भवकूटैकस्वरूपमुखपङ्कजा।। ३४ ।।

कण्ठाधःकटिपर्यन्तमध्यकूटस्वरूपिणी।
शक्तिकूटैकतापन्नकट्यधोभागधारिणी।। ३५ ।।

मूलमन्त्रात्मिका मूलकूटत्रयकलेबरा।
कुलामृतैकरसिका कुलसंकेतपालिनी।। ३६ ।।

कुलाङ्गना कुलान्तस्था कौलिनी कुलयोगिनी।
अकुला समयान्तस्था समयाचारतत्परा।। ३७ ।।

मूलाधारैकनिलया ब्रह्मग्रन्थिविभेदिनी।
मणिपूरान्तरुदिता विष्णुग्रन्थिविभेदिनी।। ३८ ।।

आज्ञाचक्रान्तरालस्था रुद्रग्रन्थिविभेदिनी।
सहस्राराम्बुजारूढा सुधासाराभिवर्षिणी।। ३९ ।।

तटिल्लतासमरुचिः षट्चक्रोपरि संस्थिता।
महाशक्तिः कुण्डलिनी बिसतन्तुतनीयसी।। ४० ।।

भवानी भावनागम्या भवारण्यकुठारिका।
भद्रप्रिया भद्रमूर्तिर्भक्तसौभाग्यदायिनी।। ४१ ।।

भक्तिप्रिया भक्तिगम्या भक्तिवश्या भयापहा।
शांभवी शारदाराध्या शर्वाणी शर्मदायिनी।। ४२ ।।

शांकरी श्रीकरी साध्वी शरच्चन्द्रनिभानना।
शातोदरी शान्तिमती निराधारा निरञ्जना।। ४३ ।।

निर्लेपा निर्मला नित्या निराकारा निराकुला।
निर्गुणा निष्कला शान्ता निष्कामा निरुपप्लवा।। ४४ ।।

नित्यमुक्ता निर्विकारा निष्प्रपञ्चा निराश्रया।
नित्यशुद्धा नित्यबुद्धा निरवद्या निरन्तरा।। ४५ ।।

निष्कारणा निष्कलङ्का निरुपाधिर्निरीश्वरा।
नीरागा रागमथना निर्मदा मदनाशिनी।। ४६ ।।

निश्चिन्ता निरहंकारा निर्मोहा मोहनाशिनी।
निर्ममा ममताहन्त्री निष्पापा पापनाशिनी।। ४७ ।।

निष्क्रोधा क्रोधशमनी निर्लोभा लोभनाशिनी।
निःसंशया संशयघ्नी निर्भवा भवनाशिनी।। ४८ ।।

निर्विकल्पा निराबाधा निर्भेदा भेदनाशिनी।
निर्नाशा मृत्युमथनी निष्क्रिया निष्परिग्रहा।। ४९ ।।

निस्तुला नीलचिकुरा निरपाया निरत्यया।
दुर्लभा दुर्गमा दुर्गा दुःखहन्त्री सुखप्रदा।। ५० ।।

दुष्टदूरा दुराचारशमनी दोषवर्जिता।
सर्वज्ञा सान्द्रकरुणा समानाधिकवर्जिता।। ५१ ।।

सर्वशक्तिमयी सर्वमङ्गला सद्गतिप्रदा।
सर्वेश्वरी सर्वमयी सर्वमन्त्रस्वरूपिणी।। ५२ ।।

सर्वयन्त्रात्मिका सर्वतन्त्ररूपा मनोन्मनी।
माहेश्वरी महादेवी महालक्ष्मी मृडप्रिया।। ५३ ।।

महारूपा महापूज्या महापातकनाशिनी।
महामाया महासत्त्वा महाशक्तिर्महारतिः।। ५४ ।।

महाभोगा महैश्वर्या महावीर्या महाबला।
महाबुद्धिर्महासिद्धिर्महायोगेश्वरेश्वरी।। ५५ ।।

महातन्त्रा महामन्त्रा महायन्त्रा महासना।
महायागक्रमाराध्या महाभैरवपूजिता।। ५६ ।।

महेश्वरमहाकल्पमहाताण्डवसाक्षिणी।
महाकामेशमहिषी महात्रिपुरसुन्दरी।। ५७ ।।

चतुःषष्ठ्युपचाराढ्या चतुःषष्टिकलामयी।
महाचतुःषष्टिकोटियोगिनीगणसेविता।। ५८ ।।

मनुविद्या चन्द्रविद्या चन्द्रमण्डलमध्यगा।
चारुरूपा चारुहासा चारुचन्द्रकलाधरा।। ५९ ।।

चराचरजगन्नाथा चक्रराजनिकेतना।
पार्वती पद्मनयना पद्मरागसमप्रभा।। ६० ।।

पञ्चप्रेतासनासीना पञ्चब्रह्मस्वरूपिणी।
चिन्मयी परमानन्दा विज्ञानघनरूपिणी।। ६१ ।।

ध्यानध्यातृध्येयरूपा धर्माधर्मविवर्जिता।
विश्वरूपा जागरिणी स्वपन्ती तैजसात्मिका।। ६२ ।।

सुप्ता प्राज्ञात्मिका तुर्या सर्वावस्थाविवर्जिता।
सृष्टिकर्त्री ब्रह्मरूपा गोप्त्री गोविन्दरूपिणी।। ६३।।

संहारिणी रुद्ररूपा तिरोधानकरी(ई)श्वरी।
सदाशिवाऽनुग्रहदा पञ्चकृत्यपरायणा।। ६४ ।।

भानुमण्डलमध्यस्था भैरवी भगमालिनी।
पद्मसना भगवती पद्मनाभसहोदरी।। ६५ ।।

उन्मेषनिमिषोत्पन्नविपन्नभुवनावलिः।
सहस्त्रशीर्षवदना सहस्त्रक्षी सहस्त्रपात्।। ६६ ।।

आब्रह्मकीटजननी वर्णाश्रमविधायिनी।
निजाज्ञारूपनिगमा पुण्यापुण्यफलप्रदा।। ६७ ।।

श्रुतिसीमन्तसिन्दूरीकृतपादाब्जधूलिका।
सकलागमसंदोहशुक्तिसंपुटमौक्तिका।। ६८ ।।

पुरुषार्थप्रदा पूर्णा भोगिनी भुवनेश्वरी।
अम्बिकाऽनादिनिधना हरिब्रह्मेन्द्रसेविता।। ६९ ।।

नारायणी नादरूपा नामरूपविवर्जिता।
ह्रीङ्कारी ह्रीमती हृद्या हेयोपादेयवर्जिता।। ७० ।।

राजराजार्चिता राज्ञी रम्या राजीवलोचना।
रञ्जनी रमणी रस्या रणत्किङ्किणिमेखला।। ७१ ।।

रमा राकेन्दुवदना रतिरूपा रतिप्रिया।
रक्षाकरी राक्षसघ्नी रामा रमणलम्पटा।। ७२ ।।

काम्या कामकलारूपा कदम्बकुसुमप्रिया।
कल्याणी जगतीकन्दा करुणारससागरा।। ७३ ।।

कलावती कलालापा कान्ता कादम्बरीप्रिया।
वरदा वामनयना वारुणीमदविह्वला।। ७४ ।।

विश्वाधिका वेदवेद्या विन्ध्याचलनिवासिनी।
विधात्री वेदजननी विष्णुमाया विलासिनी ।। ७५ ।।

क्षेत्रस्वरूपा क्षेत्रेशी क्षेत्रक्षेत्रज्ञपालिनी।
क्षयवृद्धिविनिर्मुक्ता क्षेत्रपालसमर्चिता।। ७६ ।।

विजया विमला वन्द्या वन्दारुजनवत्सला।
वाग्वादिनी वामकेशी वह्निमण्डलवासिनी।। ७७ ।।

भक्तिमत्कल्पलतिका पशुपाशविमोचिनी।
संहृताशेषपाषण्डा सदाचारप्रवर्तिका।। ७८ ।।

तापत्रयाग्निसंतप्तसमाह्लादनचन्द्रिका।
तरुणी तापसाराध्या तनुमध्या तमोऽपहा।। ७९ ।

चितिस्तत्पदलक्ष्यार्था चिदेकरसरूपिणी।
स्वात्मानन्दलवीभूतब्रह्माद्यानन्दसंततिः।। ८० ।।

परा प्रत्यक्चितीरूपा पश्यन्ती परदेवता।
मध्यमा वैखरीरूपा भक्तमानसहंसिका।। ८१ ।।

कामेश्वरप्राणनाडी कृतज्ञा कामपूजिता।
शृङ्गाररससम्पूर्णा जया जालन्धरस्थिता।। ८२ ।।

ओड्याणपीठनिलया बिन्दुमण्डलवासिनी।
रहोयागक्रमाराध्या रहस्तर्पणतर्पिता।। ८३ ।।

सद्यःप्रसादिनी विश्वसाक्षिणी साक्षिवर्जिता।
षडङ्गदेवतायुक्ता षाड्गुण्यपरिपूरिता।। ८४ ।।

नित्यक्लिन्ना निरुपमा निर्वाणसुखदायिनी।
नित्याषोडशिकारूपा श्रीकण्ठार्धशरीरिणी।। ८५ ।।

प्रभावती प्रभारूपा प्रसिद्धा परमेश्वरी।
मूलप्रकृतिरव्यक्ता व्यक्ताव्यक्तस्वरूपिणी।। ८६ ।।

व्यापिनी विविधाकारा विद्याविद्यास्वरूपिणी।
महाकामेशनयनकुमुदाह्लादकौमुदी।। ८७ ।।

भक्तहार्दतमोभेदभानुमद्भानुसन्ततिः।
शिवदूती शिवाराध्या शिवमूर्तिः शिवंकरी।। ८८ ।।

शिवप्रिया शिवपरा शिष्टेष्टा शिष्टपूजिता।
अप्रमेया स्वप्रकाशा मनोवाचामगोचरा।। ८९ ।।

चिच्छक्तिश्चेतनारूपा जडशक्तिर्जडात्मिका।
गायत्री व्याहृतिः संध्या द्विजवृंदनिषेविता।। ९० ।।

तत्त्वासना तत्त्वमयी (तत् त्वम् अयी) पञ्चकोशान्तरस्थिता।
निःसीममहिमा नित्ययौवना मदशालिनी।। ९१ ।।

मदघूर्णितरक्ताक्षी मदपाटलगण्डभूः।
चन्दनद्रवदिग्धाङ्गी चाम्पेयकुसुमप्रिया।। ९२ ।।

कुशला कोमलाकारा कुरुकुल्ला कुलेश्वरी।
कुलकुण्डालया कौलमार्गतत्परसेविता।। ९३।।

कुमारगणनाथाम्बा तुष्टिः पुष्टिर्मतिर्धृतिः।
शान्तिः स्वस्तिमती कान्तिर्नन्दिनी विघ्ननाशिनी।। ९४ ।।

तेजोवती त्रिनयना लोलाक्षी कामरूपिणी।
मालिनी हंसिनी माता मलयाचलवासिनी।। ९५ ।।

सुमुखी नलिनी सुभ्रूः शोभना सुरनायिका।
कालकण्ठी कान्तिमती क्षोभिणी सूक्ष्मरूपिणी।। ९६ ।।

वज्रेश्वरी वामदेवी वयोऽवस्थाविवर्जिता।
सिद्धेश्वरी सिद्धविद्या सिद्धमाता यशस्विनी।। ९७ ।।

विशुद्धचक्रनिलयाऽऽरक्तवर्णा त्रिलोचना।
खट्वाङ्गादिप्रहरणा वदनैकसमन्विता।। ९८ ।।

पायसान्नप्रिया त्वक्स्था पशुलोकभयङ्करी।
अमृतादिमहाशक्तिसंवृता डाकिनीश्वरी।। ९९ ।।

अनाहताब्जनिलया श्यामाभवदनद्वया।
दंष्ट्रोज्ज्वलाऽक्षमालादिधरा रुधिरसंस्थिता।। १००।।

कालरात्र्यादिशक्त्यौघवृता स्निग्धौदनप्रिया।
महावीरेन्द्रवरदा राकिण्यम्बास्वरूपिणी।। १०१ ।।

मणिपूराब्जनिलया वदनत्रयसंयुता।
वज्रादिकायुधोपेता डामर्यादिभिरावृता।। १०२ ।।

रक्तवर्णा मांसनिष्ठा गुडान्नप्रीतमानसा।
समस्तभक्तसुखदा लाकिन्यम्बास्वरूपिणी।। १०३ ।।

स्वाधिष्ठानाम्बुजगता चतुर्वक्त्रमनोहरा।
शूलाद्यायुधसंपन्ना पीतवर्णाऽतिगर्विता।। १०४ ।।

मेदोनिष्ठा मधुप्रीता बन्दिन्यादिसमन्विता।
दध्यन्नासक्तहृदया काकिनीरूपधारिणी।। १०५ ।।

मूलाधाराम्बुजारूढा पञ्चवक्त्राऽस्थिसंस्थिता।
अङ्कुशादिप्रहरणा वरदादिनिषेविता।। १०६ ।।

मुद्गौदनासक्तचित्ता साकिन्यम्बास्वरूपिणी।
आज्ञाचक्राब्जनिलया शुक्लवर्णा षडानना।। १०७ ।।

मज्जासंस्था हंसवती मुख्यशक्तिसमन्विता।
हरिद्रान्नैकरसिका हाकिनीरूपधारिणी।। १०८ ।।

सहस्रदलपद्मस्था सर्ववर्णोपशोभिता।
सर्वायुधधरा शुक्लसंस्थिता सर्वतोमुखी।। १०९ ।।

सर्वौदनप्रीतचित्ता याकिन्यम्बास्वरूपिणी।
स्वाहा स्वधामतिर्मेधा श्रुतिः स्मृति-रनुत्तमा।। ११० ।।

पुण्यकीर्तिः पुण्यलभ्या पुण्यश्रवणकीर्तना।
पुलोमजार्चिता बन्धमोचनी बर्ब(बन्धु)रालका।। १११ ।।

विमर्शरूपिणी विद्या वियदादिजगत्प्रसूः।
सर्वव्याधिप्रशमनी सर्वमृत्युनिवारिणा।। ११२ ।।

अग्रगण्याचिन्त्यरूपा कलिकल्मषनाशिनी।
कात्यायनी कालहन्त्री कमलाक्षनिषेविता।। ११३ ।।

ताम्बूलपूरितमुखी दाडिमीकुसुमप्रभा।
मृगाक्षी मोहिनी मुख्या मृडानी मित्ररूपिणी।। ११४ ।।

नित्यतृप्ता भक्तनिधिर्नियन्त्री निखिलेश्वरी।
मैत्र्यादिवासनालभ्या महाप्रलयसाक्षिणी।। ११५ ।।

परा शक्तिः परा निष्ठा प्रज्ञानघनरूपिणी।
माध्वीपानालसा मत्ता मातृकावर्णरूपिणी।। ११६ ।।

महाकैलासनिलया मृणालमृदुदोर्लता।
महनीया दयामूर्तिर्महासाम्राज्यशालिनी।। ११७।।

आत्मविद्या महाविद्या श्रीविद्या कामसेविता।
श्रीषोडशाक्षरीविद्या त्रिकूटा कामकोटिका।। ११८ ।।

कटाक्षकिङ्करीभूतकमलाकोटिसेविता।
शिरःस्थिता चन्द्रनिभा फालस्थेन्द्रधनुःप्रभा।। ११९ ।।

हृदयस्था रविप्रख्या त्रिकोणान्तरदीपिका।
दाक्षायणी दैत्यहन्त्री दक्षयज्ञविनाशिनी।। १२० ।।

दरान्दोलितदीर्घाक्षी दरहासोज्ज्वलन्मुखी।
गुरुमूर्तिर्गुणनिधिर्गोमाता गुहजन्मभूः।। १२१ ।।

देवेशी दण्डनीतिस्था दहराकाशरूपिणी।
प्रतिपन्मुख्यराकान्ततिथिमण्डलपूजिता।। १२२ ।।

कलात्मिका कलानाथा काव्यालापविनोदिनी।
सचामररमावाणीसव्यदक्षिणसेविता।। १२३ ।।

आदिशक्तिरमेयात्मा परमा पावनाकृतिः।
अनेककोटिब्रह्माण्डजननी दिव्यविग्रहा।। १२४ ।।

क्लींकारी केवला गुह्या कैवल्यपददायिनी।
त्रिपुरा त्रिजगद्वन्द्या त्रिमूर्तिस्त्रिदशेश्वरी।। १२५ ।।

त्र्यक्षरी दिव्यगन्धाढ्या सिन्दूरतिलकाञ्चिता।
उमा शैलेन्द्रतनया गौरी गन्धर्वसेविता।। १२६ ।।

विश्वगर्भा स्वर्णगर्भावरदा वागधीश्वरी।
ध्यानगम्यापरिच्छेद्या ज्ञानदा ज्ञानविग्रहा।। १२७ ।।

सर्ववेदान्तसंवेद्या सत्यानन्दस्वरूपिणी।
लोपामुद्रार्चिता लीलाक्लृप्तब्रह्माण्डमण्डला।। १२८ ।

अदृश्या दृश्यरहिता विज्ञात्री वेद्यवर्जिता।
योगिनी योगदा योग्या योगानन्दा युगंधरा।। १२९ ।।

इच्छाशक्तिज्ञानशक्तिक्रियाशक्तिस्वरूपिणी।
सर्वाधारा सुप्रतिष्ठा सदसद्रूपधारिणी।। १३० ।।

अष्टमूर्तिरजाजैत्री लोकयात्राविधायिनी।
एकाकिनी भूमरूपा निर्द्वैता द्वैतवर्जिता।। १३१ ।।

अन्नदा वसुदा वृद्धा ब्रह्मात्मैक्यस्वरूपिणी।
बृहती ब्राह्मणी ब्राह्मी ब्रह्मानन्दा बलिप्रिया।। १३२ ।।

भाषारूपा बृहत्सेना भावाभावविवर्जिता।
सुखाराध्या शुभकरी शोभनासुलभा गतिः।। १३३ ।।

राजराजेश्वरी राज्यदायिनी राज्यवल्लभा।
राजत्कृपा राजपीठनिवेशितनिजाश्रिता।। १३४ ।।

राज्यलक्ष्मीः कोशनाथा चतुरङ्गबलेश्वरी।
साम्राज्यदायिनी सत्यसंधा सागरमेखला।। १३५।।

दीक्षिता दैत्यशमनी सर्वलोकवशंकरी।
सर्वार्थदात्री सावित्री सच्चिदानन्दरूपिणी।। १३६ ।।

देशकालापरिच्छिन्ना सर्वगा सर्वमोहिनी।
सरस्वती शास्त्रमयी गुहाम्बा गुह्यरूपिणी।। १३७ ।।

सर्वोपाधिविनिर्मुक्ता सदाशिवपतिव्रता।
सम्प्रदायेश्वरी साध्वी गुरुमण्डलरूपिणी ।। १३८ ।।

कुलोत्तीर्णा भगाराध्या माया मधुमती मही।
गणाम्बा गुह्यकाराध्या कोमलाङ्गी गुरुप्रिया।। १३९ ।।

स्वतन्त्रा सर्वतन्त्रेशी दक्षिणामूर्तिरूपिणी।
सनकादिसमाराध्या शिवज्ञानप्रदायिनी ।। १४० ।।

चित्कलानन्दकलिका प्रेमरूपा प्रियंकरी।
नामपरायणप्रीता नन्दिविद्या नटेश्वरी।। १४१ ।।

मिथ्याजगदधिष्ठाना मुक्तिदा मुक्तिरूपिणी।
लास्यप्रिया लयकरी लज्जा रम्भादिवन्दिता।। १४२ ।।

भवदावसुधावृष्टिः पापारण्यदवानला।
दौर्भाग्यतूलवातूला जराध्वान्तरविप्रभा ।। १४३ ।।

भाग्याब्धिचन्द्रिका भक्तचित्तकेकीघनाघना।
रोगपर्वतदम्भोलिर्मृत्युदारुकुठारिका।। १४४ ।।

महेश्वरी महाकाली महाग्रासा महाशना।
अपर्णा चण्डिका चण्डमुण्डासुरनिषूदनी।। १४५ ।।

क्षाराक्षरात्मिका सर्वलोकेशी विश्वधारिणी।
त्रिवर्गदात्री सुभगा त्र्यम्बिका त्रिगुणात्मिका।। १४६ ।।

स्वर्गापवर्गदा शुद्धा जपापुष्पनिभाकृतिः।
ओजोवती द्युतिधरा यज्ञरूपा प्रियव्रता।। १४७ ।।

दुराराध्या दुराधर्षा पाटलीकुसुमप्रिया।
महती मेरुनिलया मन्दारकुसुमप्रिया।। १४८ ।।

वीराराध्या विराड्रूपा विरजा विश्वतोमुखी।
प्रत्यग्रूपा पराकाशा प्राणदा प्राणरूपिणी ।। १४९ ।।

मार्ताण्डभैरवाराध्या मन्त्रिणीन्यस्तराज्यधूः ।
त्रिपुरेशी जयत्सेना निस्त्रैगुण्या परापरा।। १५० ।।

सत्यज्ञानानन्दरूपा सामरस्यपरायणा।
कपर्दिनी कलामाला कामधुक्कामरूपिणी।। १५१।।

कलानिधिः काव्यकला रसज्ञा रसशेवधिः।
पुष्टा पुरातना पूज्या पुष्करा पुष्करेक्षणा।। १५२ ।।

परं ज्योतिः परं धाम परमाणुः परात्परा।
पाशहस्ता पाशहन्त्री परमन्त्रविभेदिनी।। १५३ ।।

मूर्तामूर्तानित्यतृप्ता मुनिमानसहंसिका।
सत्यव्रता सत्यरूपा सर्वान्तर्यामिणी सती।। १५४ ।।

ब्रह्माणी ब्रह्मजननी बहुरूपा बुधार्चिता।
प्रसवित्री प्रचण्डाज्ञा प्रतिष्ठा प्रकटाकृतिः।। १५५ ।।

प्राणेश्वरी प्राणदात्री पञ्चाशत्पीठरूपिणी।
विशृङ्खला विविक्तस्था वीरमाता वियत्प्रसूः।। १५६ ।।

मुकुन्दा मुक्तिनिलया मूलविग्रहरूपिणी।
भावज्ञा भवरोगघ्नी भवचक्रप्रवर्तिनी।। १५७ ।।

छन्दःसारा शास्त्रसारा मन्त्रसारा तलोदरी।
उदारकीर्तिरुद्दामवैभवा वर्णरूपिणी।। १५८ ।।

जन्ममृत्युजरातप्तजनविश्रान्तिदायिनी।
सर्वोपनिषदुद्घुष्टा शान्त्यतीतकलात्मिका।। १५९ ।।

गम्भीरा गगनान्तःस्था गर्विता गानलोलुपा।
कल्पनारहिता काष्ठा कान्ता कान्तार्धविग्रहा।। १६० ।।

कार्यकारणनिर्मुक्ता कामकेलितरङ्गिता।
कनत्कनकताटङ्का लीलाविग्रहधारिणी।। १६१ ।।

अजा क्षयविनिर्मुक्ता मुग्धा क्षिप्रप्रसादिनी।
अन्तर्मुखसमाराध्या बहिर्मुखसुदुर्लभा।। १६२ ।।

त्रयी त्रिवर्गनिलया त्रिस्था त्रिपुरमालिनी।
निरामया निरालम्बा स्वात्मारामा सुधासृतिः।। १६३ ।।

संसारपङ्कनिर्भग्नसमुद्धरणपण्डिता।
यज्ञप्रिया यज्ञकर्त्री यजमानस्वरूपिणी।। १६४ ।।

धर्माधारा धनाध्यक्षा धनधान्यविवर्धिनी।
विप्रप्रिया विप्ररूपा विश्वभ्रमणकारिणी।। १६५ ।।

विश्वग्रासा विद्रुमाभा वैष्णवी विष्णुरूपिणी।
अयोनिर्योनिनिलया कूटस्था कुलरूपिणी।। १६६ ।।

वीरगोष्ठीप्रिया वीरा नैष्कर्म्या नादरूपिणी।
विज्ञानकलना कल्या विदग्धा बैन्दवासना।। १६७ ।।

तत्त्वाधिका तत्त्वमयी तत्त्वमर्थस्वरूपिणी।
सामगानप्रिया सौम्या सदाशिवकुटुम्बिनी।। १६८ ।।

सव्यापसव्यमार्गस्था सर्वापद्विनिवारिणी।
स्वस्था स्वभावमधुरा धीरा धीरसमर्चिता।। १६९ ।।

चैतन्यार्घ्यसमाराध्या चैतन्यकुसुमप्रिया।
सदोदिता सदा तुष्टा तरुणादित्यपाटला।। १७० ।।

दक्षिणादक्षिणाराध्या दरस्मेरमुखाम्बुजा।
कौलिनीकेवलानर्घ्यकैवल्यपददायिनी।। १७१ ।।

स्तोत्रप्रिया स्तुतिमती श्रुतिसंस्तुतवैभवा।
मनस्विनी मानवती महेशी मङ्गलाकृतिः।। १७२ ।।

विश्वमाता जगद्धात्री विशालाक्षी विरागिणी।
प्रगल्भा परमोदारा परमोदा मनोमयी।। १७३ ।।

व्योमकेशी विमानस्था वज्रिणी वामकेश्वरी।
पञ्चयज्ञप्रिया पञ्चप्रेतमञ्चाधिशायिनी।। १७४ ।।

पञ्चमी पञ्चभूतेशी पञ्चसंख्योपचारिणी।
शाश्वती शाश्वतैश्वर्या शर्मदा शम्भुमोहिनी।। १७५ ।।

धरा धरसुता धन्या धर्मिणी धर्मवर्धिनी।
लोकातीता गुणातीता सर्वातीता शमाश्रिता।। १७६ ।।

बन्धूककुसुमप्रख्या बाला लीलाविनोदिनी।
सुमङ्गली सुखकरी सुवेषाढ्या सुवासिनी।। १७७ ।।

सुवासिन्यर्चनप्रीताऽऽशोभना शुद्धमानसा।
बिन्दुतर्पणसंतुष्टा पूर्वजा त्रिपुराम्बिका।। १७८ ।।

दशमुद्रासमाराध्या त्रिपुराश्रीवशङ्करी।
ज्ञानमुद्रा ज्ञानगम्या ज्ञानज्ञेयस्वरूपिणी।। १७९ ।।

योनिमुद्रा त्रिखण्डेशी त्रिगुणाम्बा त्रिकोणगा।
अनघाऽद्भुतचारित्रा वाञ्छितार्थप्रदायिनी।। १८० ।।

अभ्यासातिशयज्ञाता षडध्वातीतरूपिणी।
अव्याजकरुणामूर्तिरज्ञानध्वान्तदीपिका।। १८१ ।।

आबालगोपविदिता सर्वानुल्लङ्घ्यशासना।
श्रीचक्रराजनिलया श्रीमत्त्रिपुरसुन्दरी।। १८२ ।।

श्रीशिवाशिवशक्त्यैक्यरूपिणी ललिताम्बिका।
श्रीमणिसध्रींविविधगुडदरान्देशैश्च पुष्टनादाभ्याम्।
नामसु शतकारम्भा न स्तोभो नापि शब्दपुनरुक्तिः।। १८३ ।।

1. ॐ श्रीमात्रे नमः
ॐ श्रीमात्रे स्वाहा

Namaskar to the Auspicious Mother.

2. ॐ श्रीमहाराज्ञ्यै नमः
ॐ श्री-महा-राज्ञ्यै स्वाहा

Namaskar to the Supreme Sovereign – Great Queen.

3. ॐ श्रीमत्सिंहासनेश्वर्यै नमः
ॐ श्रीमत्-सिंहासनेश्वर्यै स्वाहा

Namaskar to the Ishwari, having the couch of lion as the auspicious throne.

4. ॐ चिदग्निकुण्डसम्भूतायै नमः
ॐ चित्-अग्नि-कुण्ड-सम्भूतायै स्वाहा

Namaskar to Her, who is born on the altar fire of Cit-sakti as energy of consciousness.

5. ॐ देवकार्यसमुद्यतायै नमः
ॐ देव-कार्य-समुद्यतायै स्वाहा

Namaskar to Her, who is ever conscious to work for the Devas – the brilliant gods.

6. ॐ उद्यद्भनानुसहस्राभायै नमः
ॐ उद्यद्-भानु-सहस्र-आभायै स्वाहा

Namaskar to the Mother, who has the brilliance of thousand rising suns.

7. ॐ चतुर्बाहुसमन्वितायै नमः
ॐ चतुर्बाहु-समन्वितायै स्वाहा

Namaskar to the Mother, who has four arms.

8. ॐ रागस्वरूपपाशाढ्यायै नमः
ॐ राग-स्वरूप-पाश-आढ्यायै स्वाहा

Namaskar to the Mother holding the Pasha-noose of desire (Iccha-sakti.)

9. ॐ क्रोधाकाराङ्कुशोज्जवलायै नमः

ॐ क्रोध - आकार-अंकुश-उज्जवलायै स्वाहा

Namaskar to the Moher weilding the fiery ankush - goad or elephant hook, symbolising emotion and former material existence.

10. ॐ मनोरूपेक्षुकोदण्डायै नमः

ॐ मनः-रूपेक्षु-कोदण्डायै स्वाहा

Namaskar to the Mother Creatrix, who holds the bow of sugar-cane symbolising the mental energy of Samkalpa and Vikalpa.

11. ॐ पञ्चतन्मात्रसायकायै नमः

ॐ पञ्च-तन्मात्र-सायकायै स्वाहा

Namaskar to the Mother par-excellence, who is armoured with the arrows of five subtle elements.

12. ॐ निजारूण प्रभापूरमज्जदब्रह्माण्डमण्डलायै नमः

ॐ निज-अरुण-प्रभा-पूर-मज्जद्-ब्रह्माण्ड-मण्डलायै स्वाहा

Namaskar to the Supreme Mother, who engulfs the whole universe with Her Own rosy red effulgence.

13. ॐ चम्पकाशोकपुन्नागसौगन्धिकलसत्कचायै नमः

ॐ चम्पक-अशोक-पुन्नाग-सौगन्धिक-लसत्कचायै स्वाहा

Namaskar to the most Beautiful Mother, adorned with the (flowers of) campaka, ashoka, pun-naga and saugandhika.

14. ॐ कुरुविन्दमणिश्रेणीकनत्कोटीरमण्डितायै नमः

ॐ कुरुविन्द-मणि-श्रेणी-कनत्कोटीर-मण्डितायै स्वाहा

Namaskar to Her, who is crowned with the rows of `Kuruvinda' gems and is thus seen dazling.

15. ॐ अष्टमीचन्द्रविभ्राजदलिकस्थलशौभितायै नमः

ॐ अष्टमी-चन्द्र-विभ्राजद-अलिक-स्थल-शोभितायै स्वाहा

Namaskar to Her, whose forehead is similar to the Shukla-ashtami– the eighth lunar digit.

16. ॐ मुखचन्द्रकलङ्काभ- मृगनाभिविशेषकायै नमः

ॐ मुखचन्द्र-कलङ्काभ-मृगनाभि-विशेषकायै स्वाहा

Namaskar to Her, who is adorned with the tiny mark of 'Kasturi' in her moonlike face.

17. ॐ वदनस्मरमाङ्गल्यगृहतोरणचिल्लिकायै नमः
ॐ वदन-स्मर-माङ्गल्य-गृह-तोरण-चिल्लिकायै स्वाहा

Namaskar to the All fascinating Mother, whose eyebrows are like the entrance arches of the auspicious abode of Kamadeva – the god of love.

18. ॐ वक्त्रलक्ष्मीपरीवाहचलन्मीनाभलोचनायै नमः
ॐ वक्त्र-लक्ष्मी-परीवाह-चलन्मीनाभ-लोचनायै स्वाहा

Namaskar to the beautiful face of Lalita, which is the pond of all creation and whose eyes are like those fish, playing and swimming in that pond.

19. ॐ नवचम्पकपुष्पाभनासादण्डविराजितायै नमः
ॐ नव-चम्पक-पुष्पाभ-नासादण्ड-विराजितायै स्वाहा

Namaskar to the beautiful (face of) Mother, who looks like blown champaka flower.

20. ॐ ताराकान्तितिरस्कारिनासाभरणभासुरायै नमः
ॐ तारा-कान्ति-तिरस्कारि-नासाभरण-भासुरायै स्वाहा

Namaskar to the Mother, who is shining with the jewel of her nose ornament, which excells the stars in radiance and splendour.

21. ॐ कदम्बमञ्जरीक्लृप्तकर्णपूरमनोहरायै नमः
ॐ कदम्ब-मञ्जरी-क्लृप्त-कर्णपूर-मनोहरायै स्वाहा

Namaskar to the Mother, decorated with the bunch of Kadamba flowers, worn above her ears.

22. ॐ ताटङ्.कयुगलीभूततपनोडुपमण्डलायै नमः
ॐ ताटङ्क युगली-भूत-तपनोडुप-मण्डलायै स्वाहा

Namaskar to the Mother, who has the orb of the sun and the moon in her ear ornaments.

23. ॐ पद्मरागशिलादर्शपरिभाविकपोलभुवे नमः
ॐ पद्म-राग-शिलादर्श-परिभावि-कपोल भुवे स्वाहा

Namaskar to the Mother, whose cheeks eclipse the brightness of the ruby mirror.

24. ॐ नवविद्रुमबिम्बश्रीन्यक्कारिदशनच्छदायै नमः

ॐ नव-विद्रुम-बिम्बश्री-न्यक्कारि-दशन-च्छदायै स्वाहा

Namaskar to the lips of Mother, who put to shame the shining fresh corals and Bimbha fruit.

25. ॐ शुद्धविद्याङ्कुराकारद्विजपंक्ति द्वयोज्जवलायै नमः

ॐ शुद्धविद्या-अङ्.कुर-आकार-द्विजपंक्ति –द्वयोज्जवलायै स्वाहा

Namaskar to the two rows of Mother, having the shape as of bud of pure knowledge.

26. ॐ कर्पूरवीटिकामोदसमाकर्षिदिगन्तरायै नमः

ॐ कर्पूर-वीटिकामोद-समाकर्षि-दिगन्तरायै स्वाहाः

Namaskar to the Mother, who is with the Supreme fragrance of the 'Camphor betel', which attract the Devas from all quarters.

27. ॐ निजसल्लापमाधुर्यविनिर्भर्त्सितकच्छप्यै नमः

ॐ निज-संलाप-माधुर्य-विनिर्भर्त्सित-कच्छप्यै स्वाहा

Namaskar to the Mother's melodious speech which puts to shame the Kaechapi – the flute of Sarasvati.

28. ॐ मन्दस्मितप्रभापूरमज्जत्कामेशमानसायै नमः

ॐ मन्द स्मित-प्रभापूर-मज्जत्कामेश-मानसायै स्वाहाः

Namaskar to the Mother, with the spreading radiance of her gentle and sweet smile, which drowns the mind of Kamesha – the Lord of Love.

29. ॐ अनाकलितसादृश्यचुबुकश्रीविराजितायै नमः

ॐ अनाकलित-सादृश्य-चिबुक-श्री-विराजितातै स्वाहा

Namaskar to the chin of Mother, who is illuminated, and has no comparison even in the speech of the Devas.

30. ॐ कामेशबद्धमाङ्गल्यसूत्रशोभितकन्धरायै नमः

ॐ कामेश-बद्ध-माङ्गल्य-सूत्र-शोभित-कन्धरायै स्वाहा

Namaskar to the Mother Divine adorned with the Mangalya Sutra – the marriage thread tied by Kamesh.

31. ॐ कनकाङ़गद केयूरकमनीयभुजान्वितायै नमः

ॐ कनकांगद-केयूर-कमनीय-भुजान्वितायै स्वाहा

Namaskar to the Mother adored with the golden bracelets and bangles.

32. ॐ रत्नग्रैवेयचिन्ताकलोलमुक्ताफलान्वितायै नमः

ॐ रत्न-ग्रैवेय-चिन्ताक-लोल-मुक्ता-फलान्वितायै स्वाहा

Namaskar to the two breasts of the Mother, a value offered to the priceless love of Kameshwàra.

33. ॐ कामेश्वरप्रेमरत्नमणिप्रतिपणस्तन्यै नमः

ॐ कामेश्वर-प्रेमरत्न-मणि-प्रतिपण-स्तन्यै स्वाहा

Namaskar to the Mother, who wears a neeklace of pears, jewels, precious stones, and thus the same is being meditated upon.

34. ॐ नाभ्यालवालरोमालिलताफलकुचद्वय्यै नमः

ॐ नाभ्यालवाल-रोमालिलता-फल-कुचद्वय्ये स्वाहा

Namaskar to the Mother, having two breasts, which are like the fruit of a creeper-like hair spreading upwards from her naval.

35. ॐ लक्ष्यरोमलताधारतासमुन्नेयमध्यमायै नमः

ॐ लक्ष्य-रोम-लताधारता-समुन्नेय-मध्यमायै स्वाहा

Namaskar to the Mother's waist that can be inferred only from the above creeper of hair.

36. ॐ स्तनभारदलन्मध्यपट्टबन्धवलित्रयायै नमः

ॐ स्तन-भार-दलन्-मध्य-पट्ट-बन्ध-वलि-त्रयायै स्वाहा

Namaskar to the Mother's golden belt that supports her waist, which gives way under the weight of her breasts and makes visible the three-fold silk bands.

37. ॐ अरुणारुणकौसुम्भवस्त्रभास्वत्कटीतट्ये नमः

ॐ अरुणारुण-कौसुम्भ-वस्त्र-भास्वत् कटी-तट्यै स्वाहा

Namaskar to the shining mid region of the Mother's body, which is covered with a rosy tinted garment.

38. ॐ रत्नकिङ्किणिकारम्यरशनादामभूषितायै नमः

ॐ रत्न-किङ्किणिका-रम्य-रशना-दाम-भूषितायै स्वाहा

Namaskar to Her, who is adorned with a girdle of jewelled bells.

39. ॐ कामेशज्ञातसौभाग्यमार्दवोरुद्वयान्वितायै नमः

ॐ कामेश-ज्ञात-सौभाग्य-मार्दवोरू-द्वयान्वितायै स्वाहा

Namaskar to the Mother, having the charming and smooth thighs, which are known only by Kamesha.

40. ॐ माणिक्यमुकुटाकारजानुद्वयविराजितायै नमः
ॐ माणिक्य-मुकुट-आकार-जानु-द्वय-विराजितायै स्वाहा

Namaskar to Her having knees, which look like crowns cut to shape from Manikya–precious jewels.

41. ॐ इन्द्रगोपपरिक्षिप्तस्मरंतूणाभजङ्घि कायै नमः
ॐ इन्द्र-गोप-परिक्षिप्त-स्मरं-तूणाभ-जङ्घिकायै स्वाहा

Namaskar to the Mother's calves, which are like the quiver of Cupid that bear the decoration of sapphire.

42. ॐ गूढगुल्फायै नमः
ॐ गूढ-गुल्फायै स्वाहा

Namaskar to the Mother, whose ankles are fleshy, hence hidden.

43. ॐ कूर्मपृष्ठजयिष्णुप्रपदान्वितायै नमः
ॐ कूर्म-पृष्ठ-जयिष्णु-प्रपदान्वितायै स्वाहा

Namaskar to the Mother's two feet, which are arched, and convex in shape more than the back of the tortoise.

44. ॐ नखदीधितसञ्छन्नमज्जनतमोगुणायै नमः
ॐ नख-दीधित-सञ्छन्न-नमज्जन-तमोगुणायै स्वाहा

Namaskar to the Mother, who dispells Tamas–ignorance of her devotees, with the radiance of nails.

45. ॐ पदद्वयप्रभाजालपराकृतसरोरुहायै नमः
ॐ पद-द्वय-प्रजा-जाल-पराकृत-सरोरुहायै स्वाहा

Namaskar to the Mother, whose beautiful and captivating feet put lotus to shame.

46. ॐ सिञ्जानमणिमञ्जीरमण्डितश्रीपदाम्बुजायै नमः
ॐ सिञ्जान-मणि-मञ्जीर-मण्डित-श्री पदाम्बुजायै स्वाहा

Namaskar to the lotus feet of the Mother, which are adorned with jewelled anklets that twinkle.

47. ॐ मरालीमन्दगमनायै नमः
ॐ मराली-मन्द-गमनायै स्वाहा

Namaskar to the Mother's gait, which is gracefully slow as that of a swan.

48. ॐ महालावण्यश्रेवधये नमः
ॐ महा-लावण्य-शेवधये स्वाहा

Namaskar to the beautiful Mother, holding the treasure house of beauty.

49. ॐ सर्वारुणायै नमः
ॐ सर्व-अरुणायै स्वाहा

Namaskar to the Mother, who is all rosy red in all form.

50. ॐ अनवद्याङ्ग यै: :नमः
ॐ अनवद्याङ्गयै स्वाहा

Namaskar to each and every limb of the Mother, that is faultless hence a combination of perfection.

51. ॐ सर्वाभरणभूषितायै नमः
ॐ सर्व-आभरण-भूषितायै स्वाहा

Namaskar to the Mother, who is adorned with all ornaments.

52. ॐ शिवकामेश्वराङ्क स्थायै नमः
ॐ शिव-कामेश्वराङ्क-स्थायै स्वाहा

Namaskar to the Mother par-excellence, who rests on the lap of Shivkamesha.

53. ॐ शिवायै नमः
ॐ शिवायै स्वाहा

Namaskar to the Eternally beneficial Mother Shiva.

54. ॐ स्वाधीनवल्लभायैं नमः
ॐ स्वाधीन-वल्लभायै स्वाहा

Namaskar to the Mother, who has won over her Lord.

55. ॐ सुमेरुमध्यश्रृङ्ग स्थायै नमः
ॐ सुमेरु-मध्य-श्रृङ्गस्थायै स्वाहा

Namaskar to the Mother, who dwells on the mid-beak of Mount Sumeru.

56. ॐ श्रीमन्नगरनायिकायै नमः
ॐ श्रीमन्-नगर-नायिकायै स्वाहा

Namaskar to the revered Mother, who is the ruler of the beautiful and prosperous city.

57. ॐ चिन्तामणिगृहान्तस्थायै नमः
ॐ चिन्तामणि-गृहान्तस्थायै स्वाहा

Namaskar to the Mother, who resides in the house built of Chintamani jewel.

58. ॐ पञ्चब्रह्मासनस्थितायै नमः
ॐ पञ्च-ब्रह्मासन-स्थितायै स्वाहा

Namaskar to the Mother, who has five Brahmas – Brahma, Vishnu, Rudra, Ishan and Indra functioning as her Seat.

59. ॐ महापद्माटवीसंस्थायै नमः
ॐ महा-पद्माटवी-संस्थायै स्वाहा

Namaskar to the Mother, who dwells in the great and expensive forest of lotuses.

60. ॐ कदम्बवनवासिन्यै नमः
ॐ कदम्ब-वन-वासिन्यै स्वाहा

Namaskar to the Mother, who resides in a grove of Kadamba trees.

61. ॐ सुधासागरमध्यस्थायै नमः
ॐ सुधा-सागर-मध्यस्थायै स्वाहा

Namaskar to the Divine Mother, whose dwelling place is the centre of the ocean of nectar.

62. ॐ कामाक्ष्यै नमः
ॐ कामाक्ष्यै स्वाहा

Namaskar to the Mother with lovely eyed and whose eyes are Kama-in its own being.

63. ॐ कामदायिन्यै नमः
ॐ काम-दायिन्यै स्वाहा

Namaskar to the Mother–the fulfiller of desires.

64. ॐ देवर्षिगणसंघातस्तूयमानात्मवैभवायै नमः

ॐ देवर्षि-गण-संघात-स्तूय-आत्म-वैभवायै स्वाहा

Namaskar to the Mother, who is ever praised by the hosts of assembled Devas and Rishis.

65. ॐ भण्डासुरवधोद्युक्तशक्तिसेनासमन्वितायै नमः

ॐ भण्डासुर-वधोद्युक्त-शक्ति-सेना-समन्वितायै स्वाहा

Namaskar to the Mother, who is endowed with an army of Shaktis to slay Bhandasura, the demon.

66. ॐ सम्पत्करीसमारूढ़सिंधुरव्रजसेवितायै नमः

ॐ सम्पत्-करी-समारूढ़-सिंधुर-व्रज-सेवितायै स्वाहा

Namaskar to the Mother, who is served by Sampakari, the leader of the elephant Division of her army.

67. ॐ अश्वारूढ़ाधिष्ठिताश्वकोटिभिरावृतायै नमः

ॐ अश्वारूढ़-अधिष्ठित-अश्व-कोटिभिर्-आवृतायै स्वाहा

Namaskar to the Mother, who is encircled by the Devi Ashvarudha, the commander of the multi-crores of horse riding women soldiers.

68. ॐ चक्रराजरथारूढ़सर्वायुधपरिष्कृतायै नमः

ॐ चक्र-राज-रथारूढ़-सर्वायुध-परिष्कृतायै स्वाहा

Namaskar to the Mother having the excellent chariot 'Chakra-raj' carrying all kinds of weapons.

69. ॐ गेयचक्ररथारूढ़मन्त्रिणीपरिसेवितायै नमः

ॐ गेयचक्र-रथारूढ़-मन्त्रिणी परिसेवितायै स्वाहा

Namaskar to the Mother attended by 'Mantrini'–the dusky-coloured Shyamala Devi, and seated in the chariot Geyachakra–Shrichakra.

70. ॐ किरिचक्ररथारूढ़दण्डनाथापुरस्कृतायै नमः

ॐ किरिचक्र-रथारूढ़-दण्डनाथा-पुरस्कृतायै स्वाहा

Namaskar to the Mother, who is proceeded by Dandanatha, holding the rod of authority and riding the chariot–Kirichara or Srishtichakra.

71. ॐ ज्वालामालिनिकाक्षिप्तवह्नि प्राकारमध्यगायै नमः

ॐ ज्वाला-मालिनिकाक्षिप्त-वह्नि-प्राकार-मध्यगायै स्वाहा

Namaskar to the Mother, who rests in the centre of the garland of fire, devised by Jvala-malinika.

72. ॐ भण्डसैन्यवधोद्युक्तशक्तिविक्रमहर्षितायै नमः
ॐ भण्ड-सैन्य-वद्योद्युक्त-शक्ति-विक्रम-हर्षितायै स्वाहा

Namaskar to the Mother, who is delighted at the activity of Shaktis that are prepared to destroy the army of Bhandasura.

73. ॐ नित्यापराक्रमाटोपनिरीक्षणसमुत्सुकायै नमः
ॐ नित्या-पराक्रम्-आटोप-निरीक्षण-समुत्सुकायै स्वाहा

Namaskar to the Mother, who rejoices at noticing the valour and spirit of the Nitya Devis.

74. ॐ भण्डपुत्रवधोद्युक्तबालाविक्रमनन्दितायै नमः
ॐ भण्ड-पुत्र-वधोद्युक्त-बाला-विक्रम-नन्दितायै स्वाहा

Namaskar to the Mother, who gets delighted when her daughter Bala Devi was ready to slay the son of Bhandasura.

75. ॐ मन्त्रिण्यम्बाविरचित विषङ्ग वधतोषितायै नमः
ॐ मन्त्रिणी-अम्बा-विरचित-विषङ्ग वधतोषितायै स्वाहा

Namaskar to the Mother, who is delighted at the destruction of Vishanga accomplished by mother Mautrini.

76. ॐ विशुक्रप्राणहरणवाराही वीर्य नन्दितायै नमः
ॐ विशुक्र-प्राण-हरण-वाराही-वीर्य-नन्दितायै स्वाहा

Namaskar to the Mother, who is satisfied with the destructive power of Varahi, who killed the (second brother) of Bhandasura. His name was Vishukra.

77. ॐ कामेश्वरमुखालोककल्पितश्रीगणेश्वरायै नमः
ॐ कामेश्वर-मुखालोक-कल्पित-श्री-गणेश्वरायै स्वाहा

Namaskar to the Mother- the Creator of Shri Ganesha, with the power of her glance at the face of Kameshvara.

78. ॐ महागणेशनिर्भिन्न विघनयन्त्र प्रहर्षितायै नमः
ॐ महागणेश-निर्भिन्न-विघन-यन्त्र-प्रहर्षितायै स्वाहा

Namaskar to the Mother, who is highly delighted at Maha Ganesha's power of breaking the obstacle formed of the magic figure–The Jayavighna.

79. ॐ भण्डासुरेन्द्रनिर्भुक्तशस्त्रप्रत्यस्त्रवर्षिण्यै नमः
ॐ भण्डासुरेन्द्रनिर्भुक्त-शस्त्र-प्रत्यस्त्र-वर्षिण्यै स्वाहा

Namaskar to the Mother, who is showering missiles in the encounter with the weapons thrown by Bhandasura.

80. ॐ कराङ्गलिनखोत्पन्ननारायणदशाकृत्यै नमः
ॐ कराङ्गुलि-नखोत्न्न-नारायण-दशाकृत्यै स्वाहा

Namaskar to the Mother, who created Narayana again from her finger nails, thus formed again the ten incarnations of Narayana.

81. ॐ महापाशुपतास्त्राग्निनिर्दग्धासुरसैनिकायै नमः
ॐ महा-पाशुपत-अस्त्र-अग्नि-निर्दग्ध-सुर-सैनिकायै स्वाहा

Namaskar to the Mother, who burnt the army of Asuras, with her Astra-missile Maha Pashupat.

82. ॐ कामेश्वरास्त्रनिर्दग्ध सभण्डासुरशून्यकायै नमः
ॐ कामेश्वर-अस्त्र-निर्दग्ध-सभण्डासुर-शून्यकायै स्वाहा

Namaskar to the Mother, who with the fire of Kameshvara Astra burnt the army of Bhandasura, along with his capital cit Shunyaka.

83. ॐ ब्रह्मोपेन्द्रमहेन्द्रादिदेवसंस्तुतवैभवायै नमः
ॐ ब्रह्मा-उपेन्द्र-महेन्द्र-आदिदेव-संस्तुत-वैभवायै स्वाहा

Namaskar to the Mother, whose Supreme power is praised highly by Brahma, Indra the junior, Indra the senior and other Devatas.

84. ॐ हरनेत्राग्निसंदग्धकामसंजीवनौषध्यै नमः
ॐ हरनेत्राग्नि-संदग्ध-काम-संजीवन्-औषध्यै स्वाहा

Namaskar to the Mother with the potent Herb which brought back the life of Kamadeva, who was burnt by the fire from the third eye of Hara-the destroyer.

85. ॐ श्रीमद्वाग्भवकूटैकस्वरूपमुखपङ्कजायै नमः
ॐ श्रीमद्वाग्भव-कूट-एक-स्वरूप-मुखपङ्कजायै स्वाहा

Namaskar to the Mother's Lotus face, which represents the Divine Vagbhava group of Syllables in (the Panchadashakshari–the fifteen syllable Mantra of Devi).

86. ॐ कण्ठाधः-कटिपर्यन्तमध्यकूटस्वरूपिण्यै नमः
ॐ कण्ठाधः- कटि-पर्यन्त-मध्यकूट-स्वरूपिण्यै स्वाहा

Namaskar to the Madhyakuta formation of Her body, which is from throat to the hips. The Madhyakuta is a group of six syllables and represents the second part of Sri Vidya Mantra.

87. ॐ शक्तिकूटैकतापन्नकट्यधोभागधारिण्यै नमः
ॐ शक्ति-कूट-एक-तापन्न-कट्यधो-भाग-धारिण्यै स्वाहा

Namaskar to the Mother's Shaktikuta segment of four syllables, which is from waist downwards in her body.

88. ॐ मूलमंत्रात्मिकायै नमः
ॐ मूल-मंत्र-आत्मिकायै स्वाहा

Namaskar to the Mother, who herself is the root and spirit of Mantra.

89. ॐ मूलकूटत्रयकलेवरायै नमः
ॐ मूल-कूट-त्रय-कलेवरायै स्वाहा

Namaskar to the Mother, whose three divisions is but her own composition of existence.

90. ॐ कुलामृतैकरसिकायै नमः
ॐ कुल-अमृत-एक-रसिकायै स्वाहा

Namaskar to the Mother, who has the special taste for the nectar of 'Kula-system'

91. ॐ कुलसंकेतपालिन्यै नमः
ॐ कुल-संकेत-पालिन्यै स्वाहा

Namaskar to the Divine Mother, who protects the secrets and mysteries of the Kaula-doctrines.

92. ॐ कुलाङ्गनायै नमः
ॐ कुल-अङ्गनायै स्वाहा

Namaskar to the Holy Mother, who is ever-chaste.

93. ॐ कुलान्तस्थायै नमः
ॐ कुल-अन्तस्थायै स्वाहा

Namaskar to the Holy Mother, who resides in the inner recesses of Kula-system.

94. ॐ कौलिन्यै नमः
ॐ कौलिन्यै स्वाहा

Namaskar to the Divine Mother, who belongs to Kula–anywhere and everywhere.

95. ॐ कुलयोगिन्यै नमः
ॐ कुल-योगिन्यै स्वाहा

Namaskar to the Mother, who is in communion with Kula-yoga (the combination of knower, knowledge and what is known).

96. ॐ अकुलायै नमः
ॐ अकुलायै स्वाहा

Namaskar to the Mother, who belongs to nowhere or who has no genealogy.

97. ॐ समयान्तस्थायै नमः
ॐ समय-अन्तस्थायै स्वाहा

Namaskar to the Mother, who is worshipped through the Samaya system of Shakti tradition.

98. ॐ समयाचारतत्परायै नमः
ॐ समयाचार-तत्परायै स्वाहा

Namaskar to the Mother for whom the Samayachar system of worship is of supreme interests.

99. ॐ मूलाधारैकनिलयायै नमः
ॐ मूलाधारैक-निलयायै स्वाहा

Namaskar to the Mother, who initially resides in the Muladhara–the root of spinal cord.

100. ॐ ब्रह्मग्रन्थिविभेदिन्यै नमः
ॐ ब्रह्म-ग्रन्थि-विभेदिन्यै स्वाहा

Namaskar to the Mother, who cuts the knot known as Brahma-granthi.

101. ॐ मणिपूरान्तरुदितायै नमः
ॐ मणिपूरान्तर्-उदितायै स्वाहा

Namaskar to the Mother who appears in the Manipura – mystic chakra with ten petals.

102. ॐ विष्णुग्रन्थिविभेदिन्यै नमः
ॐ विष्णु-ग्रन्थि-विभेदिन्यै स्वाहा

Namaskar to the Mother, who breaks through Vishnu granthi.

103. ॐ आज्ञाचक्रान्तरालस्थायै नमः
ॐ आज्ञा-चक्र-अन्तरालस्थायै स्वाहा

Namaskar to the Mother, who is present in the mystic Ajnachakra.

104. ॐ रुद्रग्रन्थिविभेदिन्यै नमः
ॐ रुद्रग्रन्थि-विभेदिन्यै स्वाहा

Namaskar to the Mother, who reveres the Rudra-granthi.

105. ॐ सहस्राम्बुजारूढ़ायै नमः
ॐ सहस्र-अम्बुज-आरूढ़ायै स्वाहा

Namaskar to the Mother, who ascends the thousand-petalled lotus.

106. ॐ सुधासाराभिवर्षिण्यै नमः
ॐ सुधासार-अभिवर्षिण्यै स्वाहा

Namaskar to the Mother, who showers down torrents of ambrosia.

107. ॐ तडिल्लतासमरुच्यै नमः
ॐ तडित्-लता-समरुच्यै स्वाहा

Namaskar to the brilliance of the Mother, who is like a lightning flash.

108. ॐ षट्चक्रोपरिसंस्थितायै नमः
ॐ षट्-चक्र-उपरि-संस्थितायै स्वाहा

Namaskar to the Mother, who resides above the six chakras.

109. ॐ महासक्त्यै नमः
ॐ महासक्त्यै स्वाहा

Namaskar to the Mother, who is greatly attachad to the festivals–the union of Shiva and Shakti.

110. ॐ कुण्डलिन्यै नमः
ॐ कुण्डलिन्यै स्वाहा

Namaskar to the Mother, who resides in the Kundalini–the serpent coil or the vital energy.

111. ॐ बिसतन्तुतनीयस्यै नमः

ॐ बिस-तन्तु-तनीयस्यै स्वाहा

Namaskar to the Mother, who is fine and subtle as the fibre of the lotus stalk.

112. ॐ भवान्यै नमः

ॐ भवान्यै स्वाहा

Namaskar to the Consort of Bhava–Mahadeva.

113. ॐ भावनागम्यायै नमः

ॐ भावना-गम्यायै स्वाहा

Namaskar to the Mother, who is attained through meditation – Contemplation on Shabda and Artha – world and meaning.

114. ॐ भवारण्यकुठारिकायै नमः

ॐ भव-अरण्य-कुठारिकायै स्वाहा

Namaskar to the Mother, who acts as the woodcutter of the mundane forests –earthly existence.

115. ॐ भद्रप्रियायै नमः

ॐ भद्र-प्रियायै स्वाहा

Namaskar to the Mother, who loves everything what is auspicious.

116. ॐ भद्रमूर्त्यै नमः

ॐ भद्र-मूर्त्यै स्वाहा

Namaskar to the Mother, who is embodiment of all that is auspicious appearance.

117. ॐ भक्तसौभाग्यदायिन्यै नमः

ॐ भक्त-सौभाग्य-दायिन्यै स्वाहा

Namaskar to the Mother, who confers prosperity to the devotees.

118. ॐ भक्तिप्रियायै नमः

ॐ भक्ति-प्रियायै स्वाहा

Namaskar to the Mother, who gets delighted by devotion.

119. ॐ भक्तिगम्यायै नमः

ॐ भक्ति-गम्यायै स्वाहा

Namaskar to the Mother, who is easily approached by devotion.

120. ॐ भक्तिवश्यायै नमः
ॐ भक्ति-वश्यायै स्वाहा

Namaskar to the Mother who is made one's own by actions of ones pure devotion.

121. ॐ भयापहायै नमः
ॐ भय-अपहायै स्वाहा

Namaskar to the Mother, who removes all types of dangers.

122. ॐ शाम्भव्यै नमः
ॐ शाम्भव्यै स्वाहा

Namaskar to the consort of Shambu.

123. ॐ शारदाराध्यायै नमः
ॐ शारदा-आराध्यायै स्वाहा

Namaskar to the Mother, who is worshipped by Sharda –the Devi of learning, speech and music.

124. ॐ शर्वाण्यै नमः
ॐ शर्वाण्यै स्वाहा

Namaskar to the spouse of Sharva--whose body is the earth.

125. ॐ शर्मदायिन्यै नमः
ॐ शर्मदायिन्यै स्वाहा

Namaskar to the Mother, who confers happiness always.

126. ॐ शाङ्कर्यै नमः
ॐ शाङ्कर्यै स्वाहा

Namaskar to the Mother, who is the half portion of Shankara by becoming Jaganmata.

127. ॐ श्रीकर्यै नमः
ॐ श्रीकर्यै स्वाहा

Namaskar to the Mother, who is the spouse of Vishnu by becoming Lakshmi.

128. ॐ साध्व्यै नमः
ॐ साध्व्यै स्वाहा

Namaskar to the Mother, who is chaste and virtuous.

129. ॐ शरच्चन्द्रनिभाननायै नमः
ॐ शरत्-चन्द्र-निभाननायै स्वाहा

Namaskar to the Mother having the face like autumnal moon.

130. ॐ शातोदर्यै नमः
ॐ शातोदर्यै स्वाहा

Namaskar to the Mother, who has a slender waist.

131. ॐ शान्तिमत्यै नमः
ॐ शान्तिमत्यै स्वाहा

Namaskar to the Mother, who is the embodiment of peace.

132. ॐ निराधारायै नमः
ॐ निराधारायै स्वाहा

Namaskar to the Mother, who does not require any support.

133. ॐ निरञ्जनायै नमः
ॐ निरञ्जनायै स्वाहा

Namaskar to the stainless Mother.

134. ॐ निर्लेपायै नमः
ॐ निर्लेपायै स्वाहा

Namaskar to the Mother, who has no trace of impurity.

135. ॐ निर्मलायै नमः
ॐ निर्मलायै स्वाहा

Namaskar to the Mother, who is free from any impurity.

136. ॐ नित्यायै नमः
ॐ नित्यायै स्वाहा

Namaskar to the Eternal Mother.

137. ॐ निराकारायै नमः
ॐ निराकारायै स्वाहा

Namaskar to the formless Mother.

138. ॐ निराकुलायै नमः
ॐ निराकुलायै स्वाहा

Namaskar to the unagitated Mother.

139. ॐ निर्गुणायै नमः
ॐ निर्गुणायै स्वाहा

Namaskar to the unembodied Mother.

140. ॐ निष्कलायै नमः
ॐ निष्कलायै स्वाहा

Namaskar to the digitless Mother.

141. ॐ शान्तायै नमः
ॐ शान्तायै स्वाहा

Namaskar to the tranquil and serene Mother.

142. ॐ निष्कामायै नमः
ॐ निष्कामायै स्वाहा

Namaskar to the Mother, who has no trace of any desire.

143. ॐ निरुपप्लवायै नमः
ॐ निर्-उप्पलवायै स्वाहा

Namaskar to the Indestructible Mother.

144. ॐ नित्यमुक्तायै नमः
ॐ नित्य-मुक्तायै स्वाहा

Namaskar to the Everfree Mother.

145. ॐ निर्विकारायै नमः
ॐ निर्विकारायै स्वाहा

Namaskar to the Unchanging Mother.

146. ॐ निष्प्रपञ्चायै नमः
ॐ निष्प्रपञ्चायै स्वाहा

Namaskar to the Unextending Mother.

147. ॐ निराश्रयायै नमः
ॐ निराश्रयायै स्वाहा

Namaskar to the Bodiless Mother.

148. ॐ नित्यशुद्धायै नमः
ॐ नित्य शुद्धायै स्वाहा

Namaskar to the Everpure Mother.

149. ॐ नित्यबुद्धायै नमः
ॐ नित्य बुद्धायै स्वाहा

Namaskar to the Everwise Mother.

150. ॐ निरवद्यायै नमः
ॐ निर्-अवद्यायै स्वाहा

Namaskar to the Blameless Mother.

151. ॐ निरन्तरायै नमः
ॐ निरन्तरायै स्वाहा

Namaskar to the Compact Mother.

152. ॐ निष्कारणायै नमः
ॐ निष्कारणायै स्वाहा

Namaskar to the Mother, whose very existence is without cause.

153. ॐ निष्कलङ्कायै नमः
ॐ निष्कलङ्कायै स्वाहा

Namaskar to the Faultless Mother.

154. ॐ निरुपाधये नमः
ॐ निरुपाधये स्वाहा

Namaskar to the Limitless Mother.

155. ॐ निरीश्वरायै नमः
ॐ निरीश्वरायै स्वाहा

Namaskar to the Supreme Mother.

156. ॐ नीरागायै नमः
ॐ नीरागायै स्वाहा

Namaskar to the Mother, who is without any passion.

157. ॐ रागमथन्यै नमः
ॐ राग-मथन्यै स्वाहा

Namaskar to the Mother, who ever destroys the desires.

158. ॐ निर्मदायै नमः
ॐ निर्मदायै स्वाहा

Namaskar to the Mother, who is without any pride.

159. ॐ मदनाशिन्यै नमः
ॐ मद-नाशिन्यै स्वाहा

Namaskar to the Mother, who destroys the pride.

160. ॐ निश्चिन्तायै नमः
ॐ निश्चिन्तायै स्वाहा

Namaskar to the Mother, who is without any anxiety.

161. ॐ निरहङ्कारायै नमः
ॐ निरहङ्कारायै स्वाहा

Namaskar to the Mother, who has no trace of ego.

162. ॐ निर्मोहायै नमः
ॐ निर्मोहायै स्वाहा

Namaskar to the Mother, who is without bewilderment.

163. ॐ मोहनाशिन्यै नमः
ॐ मोह-नाशिन्यै स्वाहा

Namaskar to the Mother, who destroys bewilderment.

164. ॐ निर्ममायै नमः
ॐ निर्ममायै स्वाहा

Namaskar to the Mother, who is without self-interest or the conceit of 'mine'.

165. ॐ ममताहन्त्र्यै नमः
ॐ ममता-हन्त्रयै स्वाहा

Namaskar to the Mother, who destroys the conceit of 'mine'.

166. ॐ निष्पापायै नमः
ॐ निष्पापायै स्वाहा

Namaskar to the Mother, who is ever sinless.

167. ॐ पापनाशिन्यै नमः
ॐ पाप-नाशिन्यै स्वाहा

Namaskar to the Mother, who destroys sins.

168. ॐ निष्क्रोधायै नमः
ॐ निष्क्रोधायै स्वाहा

Namaskar to the Mother, who is without any anger.

169. ॐ क्रोधशमन्यै नमः
ॐ क्रोध-शमन्यै स्वाहा

Namaskar to the Mother, who is destroyer of anger.

170. ॐ निर्लोभायै नमः
ॐ निर्लोभायै स्वाहा

Namaskar to the Mother, who is without greed.

171 ॐ लोभनाशिन्यै नमः
ॐ लोभ-नाशिन्यै स्वाहा

Namaskar to the Mother, who destroys greed.

172. ॐ निःसंशयायै नमः
ॐ निःसंशयायै स्वाहा

Namaskar to the Mother, who is without doubt.

173. ॐ संशयध्नृयै नमः
ॐ संशयध्नृयै स्वाहा

Namaskar to the Mother, who destroys doubts.

174. ॐ निर्भवायै नमः
ॐ निर्भवायै स्वाहा

Namaskar to the Mother, who has no origin.

175. ॐ भवनाशिन्यै नमः
ॐ भव-नाशिन्यै स्वाहा

Namaskar to the Mother, who destroys the existence of Samsara - the world of perception.

176. ॐ निर्विकल्पायै नमः
ॐ निर्विकल्पायै स्वाहा

Namaskar to the Mother, who is pure consciousness.

177. ॐ निराबाधायै नमः
ॐ निराबाधायै स्वाहा

Namaskar to the Mother, who does not get disturbed.

178. ॐ निर्भेदायै नमः
ॐ निर्भेदायै स्वाहा

Namaskar to the Mother, in whom there is no difference, what soever.

179. ॐ भेदनाशिन्यै नमः
ॐ भेद नाशिन्यै स्वाहा

Namaskar to the Mother, who destroys the cognition of difference.

180. ॐ निर्नाशायै नमः
ॐ निर्नाशायै स्वाहा

Namaskar to the Insperishable Mother.

181. ॐ मृत्युमथन्यै नमः
ॐ मृत्यु-मथन्यै स्वाहा

Namaskar to the Mother, who destroys death.

182. ॐ निष्क्रियायै नमः
ॐ निष्क्रियायै स्वाहा

Namaskar to the Mother, who has no action.

183. ॐ निष्परिग्रहायै नमः
ॐ निष्परिग्रहायै स्वाहा

Namaskar to the Mother, who accepts nothing, as she is the bestower of everything.

184. ॐ निस्तुलायै नमः
ॐ निस्तुलायै स्वाहा

Namaskar to the Incomparable Mother.

185. ॐ नीलचिकुरायै नमः
ॐ नीलचिकुरायै स्वाहा

Namaskar to the Mother, having shining blue locks.

186. ॐ निरपायायै नमः
ॐ निरपायायै स्वाहा

Namaskar to the Imperishable Mother, who never departs.

187. ॐ निरत्ययायै नमः
ॐ निरत्ययायै स्वाहा

Namaskar to the Mother, who is without transgression.

188. ॐ दुर्लभायै नमः
ॐ दुर्लभायै स्वाहा

Namaskar to the Mother, who is difficult to attain.

189. ॐ दुर्गमायै नमः
ॐ दुर्गमायै स्वाहा

Namaskar to the Mother Durgama, as she is not easily accessible.

190. ॐ दुर्गायै नमः
ॐ दुर्गायै स्वाहा

Namaskar to the Mother Durga – a nine year old girl.

191. ॐ दुःखहन्त्र्यै नमः
ॐ दुःख-हन्त्र्यै स्वाहा

Namaskar to the Mother, who destroys pain.

192. ॐ सुखप्रदायै नमः
ॐ सुख-प्रदायै स्वाहा

Namaskar to the Mother, who confers happiness.

193. ॐ दुष्टदूरायै नमः
ॐ दुष्ट-दूरायै स्वाहा

Namaskar to the Mother, who is not attainable by sinners.

194. ॐ दुराचारशमन्यै नमः
ॐ दुराचार-शमन्यै स्वाहा

Namaskar to the Mother, who puts an end to evil customs.

195. ॐ दोषवर्जितायै नमः
ॐ दोष-वर्जितायै स्वाहा

Namaskar to the Mother, who is devoid of faults.

196. ॐ सर्वज्ञायै नमः
ॐ सर्वज्ञायै स्वाहा

Namaskar to the Omniscient Mother.

197. ॐ सान्द्रकरुणायै नमः

ॐ सान्द्र-करुणायै स्वाहा

Namaskar to the Intensely Compassionate Mother.

198. ॐ समानधिकवर्जितायै नमः

ॐ समान-अधिक-वर्जितायै स्वाहा

Namaskar to the Mother, who is having neither equal, nor superior.

199. ॐ सर्वशक्तिमय्यै नमः

ॐ सर्व-शक्तिमय्यै स्वाहा

Namaskar to the Mother, who possesses all Shaktis – powers, energies and capacities.

200. ॐ सर्वमङ्गलायै नमः

ॐ सर्व-मङ्गलायै स्वाहा

Namaskar to the Mother, who possesses all good fortune and auspiciousness.

201. ॐ सदगति प्रदायै नमः

ॐ सद्-गति-प्रदायै स्वाहा

Namaskar to the Mother, who grants most excellent goal.

202. ॐ सर्वेश्वर्यै नमः

ॐ सर्वेश्वर्यै स्वाहा

Namaskar to the Supremely ruling Mother.

203. ॐ सर्वमय्यै नमः

ॐ सर्व-मय्यै स्वाहा

Namaskar to the All pervading Mothe

204. ॐ सर्वमन्त्रस्वरूपिण्यै नमः

ॐ सर्व-मन्त्र-स्वरूपिण्यै स्वाहा

Namaskar to the Mother, who is the very essence of the Mantras - combination of mystic syllables.

205. ॐ सर्वयन्त्रात्मिकायै नमः

ॐ सर्व-यन्त्र-आत्मिकायै स्वाहा

Namaskar to the Mother, who is the soul of all Yantras - mystic diagrams.

206. ॐ सर्वतन्त्ररूपायै नमः
ॐ सर्व-तन्त्ररूपायै स्वाहा

Namaskar to the Mother, who is the spirit of all Tantras – mystic technology.

207. ॐ मनोन्मन्यै नमः
ॐ मन-उन्मन्यै स्वाहा

Namaskar to the Mother, who is called Manonmani – the undifferentiated energy.

208. ॐ माहेश्वर्यै नमः
ॐ माहेश्वर्यै स्वाहा

Namaskar to the Mother, who is the consort of Maheshvara – the Parama-Shiva aspect of reality.

209. ॐ महादेव्यै नमः
ॐ महादेव्यै स्वाहा

Namaskar to the Mother, who is Great Goddess.

210. ॐ महालक्ष्म्यै नमः
ॐ महालक्ष्म्यै स्वाहा

Namaskar to the Mother, who has taken the form of Mahalakshmi – the presiding deity of the Devi cult.

211. ॐ मृडप्रियायै नमः
ॐ मृड-प्रियायै स्वाहा

Namaskar to the Mother, who is the beloved of Mrida – the protector of the universe.

212. ॐ महारूपायै नमः
ॐ महा-रूपायै स्वाहा

Namaskar to the Mother, whose form in exceedingly great.

213. ॐ महापूज्यायै नमः
ॐ महा-पूज्यायै स्वाहा

Namaskar to the Mother, who is supreme for being adored and worshipped.

214. ॐ महापातकनाशिन्यै नमः
ॐ महा-पातक-नाशिन्यै स्वाहा

Namaskar to the Mother, who removes the harms done by great sins committed by persons.

215. ॐ महामायायै नमः
ॐ महा-मायायै स्वाहा

Namaskar to the Mother, who is the creator of the cosmic-illusion.

216. ॐ महासत्त्वायै नमः
ॐ महा-सत्त्वायै स्वाहा

Namaskar to the Mother, who is the great cosmic reality.

217. ॐ महाशक्त्यै नमः
ॐ महा-शक्त्यै स्वाहा

Namaskar to the Mother, who is the great energy Herself.

218. ॐ महारत्यै नमः
ॐ महा-रत्यै स्वाहा

Namaskar to the Mother, who is the great delight.

219. ॐ महाभोगायै नमः
ॐ महा-भोगायै स्वाहा

Namaskar to the Mother having the great extension.

220. ॐ महैश्वर्यायै नमः
ॐ महैश्वर्यायै स्वाहा

Namaskar to the Mother having the great sovereignty.

221. ॐ महावीर्यायै नमः
ॐ महा-वीर्यायै स्वाहा

Namaskar to the Mother having great strength.

222. ॐ महाबलायै नमः
ॐ महा-बलायै स्वाहा

Namaskar to the Mother having great might.

223. ॐ महाबुद्ध्यै नमः
ॐ महा-बुद्ध्यै स्वाहा

Namaskar to the Mother having the great intelligence.

224. ॐ महासिद्ध्यै नमः
ॐ महा-सिद्ध्यै स्वाहा

Namaskar to the Mother having the great attainment.

225. ॐ महायोगेश्वरेश्वर्यै नमः
ॐ महा-योगेश्वर-ईश्वर्यै स्वाहा

Namaskar to the Mother being the ruler of the great rulers.

226. ॐ महातन्त्रायै नमः
ॐ महा-तन्त्रायै स्वाहा

Namaskar to the Mother of great technology.

227. ॐ महामन्त्रायै नमः
ॐ महा-मन्त्रायै स्वाहा

Namaskar to the Mother of great formula.

228. ॐ महायन्त्रायै नमः
ॐ महा-यन्त्रायै स्वाहा

Namaskar to the Mother of great diagram.

229. ॐ महासनायै नमः
ॐ महा-आसनायै स्वाहा

Namaskar to the Mother having the great seat.

230. ॐ महायागक्रमाराध्यायै नमः
ॐ महा-याग-क्रम-आराध्यायै स्वाहा

Namaskar to the Mother, who is adored and worshipped by the Mahayaga methodology of rituals.

231. ॐ महाभैरवपूजितायै नमः
ॐ महा-भैरव-पूजितायै स्वाहा

Namaskar to the Mother, who is worshipped by Mahabhairava – Param-Shiva or Mahashiva.

232. ॐ महेश्वरमहाकल्पमहाताण्डवसाक्षिण्यै नमः

ॐ महेश्वर-महा-कल्प-महा-ताण्डव-साक्षिण्यै स्वाहा

Namaskar to the Mother, who is the witness to the cosmic dance of Maheshvara in the great Kalpa-cycle of creation, preservation and dissolution.

233. ॐ महाकामेशमहिठ्यै नमः

ॐ महा-कामेश-महिठ्यै स्वाहा

Namaskar to the Mother, who is the wife of Maha-Kameshvara – the queen of the supreme king of Kama – Param – Shiva.

234. ॐ महात्रिपुरसुन्दर्यै नमः

ॐ महा-त्रिपुर-सुन्दर्यै स्वाहा

Namaskar to the Mother, who is the great Tripurasundari.

235. ॐ चतुःषष्टियुपचाराराढ्यायै नमः

ॐ चतुःषष्टि-उपाचार-आढ्यायै स्वाहा

Namaskar to the Mother, who is adored by sixty-four ceremonies.

236. ॐ चतुःषष्टिकलामय्यै नमः

ॐ चतुःषष्टि-कला-मय्यै स्वाहा

Namaskar to the Mother, the originator of sixty four branches of science.

237. ॐ महाचतुः षष्टिकोटियोगिनीगणसेवितायै नमः

ॐ महा-चतुः-षष्टि-कोटि-योगिनी-गण-सेवितायै स्वाहा

Namaskar to the Mother attended by the great sixty-four crores of bands of Yoginis.

238. ॐ मनुविद्यायै नमः

ॐ मनु-विद्यायै स्वाहा

Namaskar to the Mother, who is Herself the Manuvidya – Srividya of twelve kinds taught by Manu, Chandra, Kubera, Lopamudra, Manmatha, Agastya, Agni, Surya, Indra, Skanda, Shiva and Durvasa.

239. ॐ चन्द्रविद्यायै नमः

ॐ चन्द्र-विद्यायै स्वाहा

Namaskar to the Mother, who is Herself the Chandravidya–formula initiated by Chandra.

240. ॐ चन्द्रमण्डलमध्यगायै नमः
ॐ चन्द्र-मण्डल-मध्यगायै स्वाहा

Namaskar to the Mother, who resides in the centre of the moon's disc.

241. ॐ चारुरूपायै नमः
ॐ चारु-रूपायै स्वाहा

Namaskar to the Mother, who is of exquisite beauty and charm.

242. ॐ चारुहासायै नमः
ॐ चारु-हासायै स्वाहा

Namaskar to the Mother possessing the beautiful smile.

243. ॐ चारुचन्द्रकलाधरायै नमः
ॐ चारु-चन्द्र-कला-धरायै स्वाहा

Namaskar to the Mother wearing a beautiful crescent moon.

244. ॐ चराचरजगन्नाथायै नमः
ॐ चराचर-जगन्नाथायै स्वाहा

Namaskar to the Mother, who is the ruler of animate and inanimate worlds.

245. ॐ चक्रराजनिकेतनायै नमः
ॐ चक्र-राज-निकेतनायै स्वाहा

Namaskar to the Mother, who abides in the Srichakra.

246. ॐ पार्वत्यै नमः
ॐ पार्वत्यै स्वाहा

Namaskar to the Mother Parvati – the daughter of Mount Himavan.

247. ॐ पद्मनयनायै नमः
ॐ पद्म-नयनायै स्वाहा

Namaskar to the lotus eyed Mother.

248. ॐ पद्मरागसमप्रभायै नमः
ॐ पद्म-राग-सम-प्रभायै स्वाहा

Namaskar to the Mother, who shines in the colours of Padma–lotus, raga-red and prabha, thus illumines in the ruby.

249. ॐ पञ्चप्रेतासनासीनायै नमः

ॐ पञ्च-प्रेतासन-आसीनायै स्वाहा

Namaskar to the Mother, who is seated on the seat of fine corpses.

250. ॐ पञ्चब्रह्मस्वरूपिण्यै नमः

ॐ पञ्च-ब्रह्म-स्वरूपिण्यै स्वाहा

Namaskar to the Mother, who is the essential of five Brahmas – Brahma, Vishnu, Rudra, Ishvara and Sadashiva.

251. ॐ चिन्मय्यै नमः

ॐ चिन्मय्यै स्वाहा

Namaskar to the Mother, who is the consciousness itself.

252. ॐ परमानन्दायै नमः

ॐ परमानन्दायै स्वाहा

Namaskar to the Mother, who is verily the supreme bliss.

253. ॐ विज्ञानघनरूपिण्यै नमः

ॐ विज्ञान-घन-रूपिण्यै स्वाहा

Namaskar to the Mother, who consists in permanent intelligence.

254. ॐ ध्यानध्यातृध्येयरूपायै नमः

ॐ ध्यान-ध्यातृ-ध्येय-रूपायै स्वाहा

Namaskar to the Mother, who Herself is meditation, meditator and the objects of meditation.

255. ॐ धर्माधर्मविवर्जितायै नमः

ॐ धर्म-अधर्म-विवर्जितायै स्वाहा

Namaskar to the Mother, who is above virtue and vice.

256. ॐ विश्वरूपायै नमः

ॐ विश्व-रूपायै स्वाहा

Namaskar to the Mother, who is omnipresent.

257. ॐ जागरिण्यै नमः

ॐ जागरिण्यै स्वाहा

Namaskar to the Mother, who is in waking state.

258. ॐ स्वपन्त्यै नमः
ॐ स्वपन्त्यै स्वाहा

Namaskar to the Mother, who is in dreaming state.

259. ॐ तैजसात्मिकायै नमः
ॐ तैजस्-आत्मिकायै स्वाहा

Namaskar to the Mother, who is Taijas itself.

260. ॐ सुप्तायै नमः
ॐ सुप्तायै स्वाहा

Namaskar to the Mother, who is in the state of sleep.

261. ॐ प्राज्ञात्मिकायै नमः
ॐ प्राज्ञ-आत्मिकायै स्वाहा

Namaskar to the Mother, who is in the form of the totality of transmigration of the Jivas--ensouled life.

262. ॐ तुर्यायै नमः
ॐ तुर्यायै स्वाहा

Namaskar to the Mother, who is in the state of ecstasy.

263. ॐ सर्वावस्थाविवर्जितायै नमः
ॐ सर्व-अवस्था-विवर्जितायै स्वाहा

Namaskar to the Mother, who transcends all the states.

264. ॐ सृष्टिकर्त्र्यै नमः
ॐ सृष्टि-कर्त्र्यै स्वाहा

Namaskar to the Mother, whose function is the Creation of the world.

265. ॐ ब्रह्मरूपायै नमः
ॐ ब्रह्म-रूपायै स्वाहा

Namaskar to the Mother, who is in the form of Brahma.

266. ॐ गोप्त्र्यै नमः
ॐ गोप्त्र्यै स्वाहा

Namaskar to the Protecting Mother.

267. ॐ गोविन्दरूपिण्यै नमः

ॐ गोविन्द-रूपिण्यै स्वाहा

Namaskar to the Mother in the form of Govinda – the all-pervading.

268. ॐ संहारिण्यै नमः

ॐ संहारिण्यै स्वाहा

Namaskar to the All destroying Mother.

269. ॐ रुद्ररूपायै नमः

ॐ रुद्ररूपायै स्वाहा

Namaskar to the Mother in the form of Rudra.

270. ॐ तिरोधानकर्यै नमः

ॐ तिरोधान-कर्यै स्वाहा

Namaskar to the Mother, whose function is Concealment – disappearance.

271. ॐ ईश्वर्यै नमः

ॐ ईश्वर्यै स्वाहा

Namaskar to the All ruling Mother.

272. ॐ सदाशिवायै नमः

ॐ सदाशिवायै स्वाहा

Namaskar to the Mother who is herself 'Sadashiva' – Ever benevolence.

273. ॐ अनुग्रहदायै नमः

ॐ अनुग्रहदायै स्वाहा

Namaskar to the Mother, who confers the blessings.

274. ॐ पञ्चकृत्यपरायणायै नमः

ॐ पञ्च-कृत्य-परायणायै स्वाहा

Namaskar to the Mother, who is devoted to the five functions – creation, preservation, destruction, annihiliation and re-appearance.

275. ॐ भानुमण्डल मध्यस्थायै नमः

ॐ भानु-मण्डल-मध्यस्थायै स्वाहा

Namaskar to the Mother, who abides in the midst of the sun's disc.

276. ॐ भैरव्यै नमः

ॐ भैरव्यै स्वाहा

Namaskar to the Mother as Bhairvi.

277. ॐ भगमालिन्यै नमः

ॐ भग-मालिन्यै स्वाहा

Namaskar to the Mother wearing the garland of prosperity.

278. ॐ पद्मासनायै नमः

ॐ पद्म-आसनायै स्वाहा

Namaskar to the Mother, seated on the lotus.

279. ॐ भगवत्यै नमः

ॐ भगवत्यै स्वाहा

Namaskar to the Mother Bhagavati – supremacy, magnanimity, wisdom, dispassion, womb, fame, power, effort, desire, righteousness, prosperity and worldly concerns.

280. ॐ पद्मनाभसहोदर्यै नमः

ॐ पद्म-नाभ-सहोदर्यै स्वाहा

Namaskar to the Mother, who is the sister of Vishnu.

281. ॐ उन्मेषनिमिषोत्पन्नविपन्नभुवनावल्यै नमः

ॐ उन्मेष-निमिष-उत्पन्न-विपन्न-भुवन-आवल्यै स्वाहा

Namaskar to the Mother, who is the unwinking and eternal witness –the series of worlds created by the opening and shutting of Her eyes.

282. ॐ सहस्रशीर्षवदनायै नमः

ॐ सहस्र-शीर्ष-वदनायै स्वाहा

Namaskar to the Mother, who is thousand headed and thousand faced.

283. ॐ सहस्राक्ष्यै नमः

ॐ सहस्र-अक्ष्यै स्वाहा

Namaskar to the Mother with thousand eyes.

284. ॐ सहस्रपदे नमः

ॐ सहस्र-पदे स्वाहा

Namaskar to the Mother with thousand feet.

285. ॐ आब्रह्मकीट्जनन्यै नमः

ॐ आब्रह्म-कीट-जनन्यै स्वाहा

Namaskar to the Mother of all the creation from Brahma to tiny worm

286. ॐ वर्णाश्रमविधायिन्यै नमः

ॐ वर्णाश्रम-विधायिन्यै स्वाहा

Namaskar to the Mother, who ordains the social orders of caste and life.

287. ॐ निजाज्ञारूपनिगमायै नमः

ॐ निज-आज्ञा-रूप-निगमायै स्वाहा

Namaskar to the Mother, whose command is made intelligible through the 'Nigamas'.

288. ॐ पुण्यापुण्यफलप्रदायै नमः

ॐ पुण्यापुण्य-फल-प्रदायै स्वाहा

Namaskar to the Mother – the giver of auspicious and inauspicious results.

289. ॐ श्रुतिसीमन्तसिन्दूरीकृतपादाब्जधूलिकायै नमः

ॐ श्रुति-सीमन्त-सिन्दूरी-कृत-पादाब्ज-धूलिकायै स्वाहा

Namaskar to the Mother, whose feet dust forms the vermilion mark on the parting of the hair on the head of the Vedas.

290. ॐ सकलागमसंदोहशुक्तिसम्पुटमौक्तिकायै नमः

ॐ सकल-आगम-संदोह-शुक्ति-सम्पुट-मौक्तिकायै स्वाहा

Namaskar to the Mother, who is the priceless pearl found in the shell casket – composed of the collected scriptures.

291. ॐ पुरुषार्थप्रदायै नमः

ॐ पुरुषार्थ-प्रदायै स्वाहा

Namaskar to the Mother, who grants the objects of human existence.

292. ॐ पूर्णायै नमः

ॐ पूर्णायै स्वाहा

Namaskar to the All perfect Mother.

293. ॐ भोगिन्यै नमः
ॐ भोगिन्यै स्वाहा

Namaskar to the Mother Bhogini – perpetual bliss.

294. ॐ भुवनेश्वर्यै नमः
ॐ भुवन-ईश्वर्यै स्वाहा

Namaskar to the Mother, who rules the universe.

295. ॐ अम्बिकायै नमः
ॐ अम्बिकायै स्वाहा

Namaskar to the Mother Ambika.

296. ॐ अनादिनिधनायै नमः
ॐ अनादि-निधनायै स्वाहा

Namaskar to the Mother having neither beginning nor end.

297. ॐ हरिब्रह्मेन्द्रसेवितायै नमः
ॐ हरि-ब्रह्मा-इन्द्र-सेवितायै स्वाहा

Namaskar to the Mother attended by Hari, Brahma and Indra.

298. ॐ नारायण्यै नमः
ॐ नारायण्यै स्वाहा

Namaskar to the Mother Narayani – the consort of Narayana.

299. ॐ नादरूपायै नमः
ॐ नाद-रूपायै स्वाहा

Namaskar to the Mother in the form of sound.

300. ॐ नामरूपविवर्जितायै नमः
ॐ नामः-रूप-विवर्जितायै स्वाहा

Namaskar to the Mother, transcending name and form.

301. ॐ ह्रीङ्कार्यै नमः
ॐ ह्रीं-कार्यै स्वाहा

Namaskar to the Mother, whose function is in the mystic syllable 'Hrim'.

302. ॐ ह्रीमत्यै नमः
ॐ ह्रीमत्यै स्वाहा

Namaskar to the Mother, who is endowed with 'Hrim' – mystic modesty.

303. ॐ हृद्यायै नमः
ॐ हृद्यायै स्वाहा

Namaskar to the Mother, who abides in the heart-region.

304. ॐ हेयोपादेयवर्जितायै नमः
ॐ हेय-उपादेय-वर्जितायै स्वाहा

Namaskar to the Mother, who has nothing to accept or reject.

305. ॐ राजराजार्चितायै नमः
ॐ राज-राजार्चितायै स्वाहा

Namaskar to the Mother, who is adored by Manu and Kubera.

306. ॐ राज्ञ्यै नमः
ॐ राज्ञ्यै स्वाहा

Namaskar to the Queen Mother.

307. ॐ रम्यायै नमः
ॐ रम्यायै स्वाहा

Namaskar to the Supremely handsome Mother.

308. ॐ राजीवलोचनायै नमः
ॐ राजीव-लोचनायै स्वाहा

Namaskar to the Mother, having eyes like those of a deer.

309. ॐ रञ्जन्यै नमः
ॐ रञ्जन्यै स्वाहा

Namaskar to the delighting Mother, also who is all manifested in colour.

310. ॐ रमण्यै नमः
ॐ रमण्यै स्वाहा

Namaskar to the Mother, who 'laughs, plays and rejoices'.

311. ॐ रस्यायै नमः
ॐ रस्यायै स्वाहा

Namaskar to the most Delectable Mother.

312. ॐ रणत्किकिङ्किणिमेखलायै नमः
ॐ रणत्-किङ्किणि-मेखलायै स्वाहा

Namaskar to the Mother, who wears a girdle of tinkling bells.

313. ॐ रमायै नमः
ॐ रमायै स्वाहा

Namaskar to the Mother, in the form of Rama–Lakshmi.

314. ॐ राकेन्दुवदनायै नमः
ॐ राकेन्दु-वदनायै स्वाहा

Namaskar to the Mother, having a face like the full moon.

315. ॐ रतिरूपायै नमः
ॐ रति-रूपायै स्वाहा

Namaskar to the Mother in the form of Rati–the spouse of Kamadeva–love god.

316. ॐ रतिप्रियायै नमः
ॐ रति-प्रियायै स्वाहा

Namaskar to the Mother, who is dear to 'Rati'.

317. ॐ रक्षाकर्यै नमः
ॐ रक्षा-कर्यै स्वाहा

Namaskar to the Protecting Mother.

318. ॐ राक्षसघ्न्यै नमः
ॐ राक्षस-घ्न्यै स्वाहा

Namaskar to the Mother, who is the Slayer of Rakshasas.

319. ॐ रामायै नमः
ॐ रामायै स्वाहा

Namaskar to the Mother, who is in the form of 'Woman' or 'yoginis'.

320. ॐ रमणलम्पटायै नमः
ॐ रमण-लम्पटायै स्वाहा

Namaskar to the Mother, who is devoted to her husband.

321. ॐ काम्यायै नमः
ॐ काम्यायै स्वाहा

Namaskar to the Mother, who is to be desired.

322. ॐ कामकलारूपायै नमः
ॐ काम-कला-रूपायै स्वाहा

Namaskar to the Mother in the form of 'Kamakala'. The supreme self and manifestation.

323. ॐ कदम्बकुसुमप्रियायै नमः
ॐ कदम्ब-कुसुम-प्रियायै स्वाहा

Namaskar to the Mother, who is fond of Kadamba flowers.

324. ॐ कल्याण्यै नमः
ॐ कल्याण्यै स्वाहा

Namaskar to the Beneficent Mother.

325. ॐ जगतीकन्दायै नमः
ॐ जगती-कन्दायै स्वाहा

Namaskar to the Mother, who is the root of the world.

326. ॐ करुणारससागराय नमः
ॐ करुणा-रस-सागराय स्वाहा

Namaskar to the Mother, who is the Ocean of the waters of compassion.

327. ॐ कलावत्यै नमः
ॐ कलावत्यै स्वाहा

Namaskar to the Mother of All arts.

328. ॐ कलालापायै नमः
ॐ कला-आलापायै स्वाहा

Namaskar to the Mother, whose conversation is 'Kala'.

329. ॐ कान्तायै नमः
ॐ कान्तायै स्वाहा

Namaskar to the Beautiful Mother.

330. ॐ कादम्बरीप्रियायै नमः
ॐ कादम्बरी-प्रियायै स्वाहा

Namaskar to the Mother Sarasvati – the fond of mead – the fermented drink.

331. ॐ वरदायै नमः
ॐ वरदायै स्वाहा

Namaskar to the Mother, who grants boons.

332. ॐ वामनयनायै नमः
ॐ वाम-नयनायै स्वाहा

Namaskar to the beautiful-eyed woman.

333. ॐ वारुणीमदविह्वलायै नमः
ॐ वारुणी-मद-विह्वलायै स्वाहा

Namaskar to the Mother, who is intoxicated with date wine.

334. ॐ विश्वाधिकायै नमः
ॐ विश्व-अधिकायै स्वाहा

Namaskar to the Mother, who transcends the Universe.

335. ॐ वेदवेद्यायै नमः
ॐ वेद-वेद्यायै स्वाहा

Namaskar to the Mother known through the Vedas.

336. ॐ विन्ध्याचलनिवासिन्यै नमः
ॐ विन्ध्याचल-निवासिन्यै स्वाहा

Namaskar to the Mother, who resides in the Vindhya mountain.

337. ॐ विधात्र्यै नमः
ॐ विधात्र्यै स्वाहा

Namaskar to the Mother, who is the supporter of the Universe.

338. ॐ वेदजनन्यै नमः
ॐ वेद-जनन्यै स्वाहा

Namaskar to the Mother of the Vedas.

339. ॐ विष्णुमायायै नमः
ॐ विष्णु-मायायै स्वाहा

Namaskar to the Vishnumaya Mother – All pervasive limiting Vishnu.

340. ॐ विलासिन्यै नमः
ॐ विलासिन्यै स्वाहा

Namaskar to the Playful Mother.

341. ॐ क्षेत्रस्वरूपायै नमः
ॐ क्षेत्र-स्वरूपायै स्वाहा

Namaskar to the Mother, who Herself is the form of Kshetra–material existence.

342. ॐ क्षेत्रेश्यै नमः
ॐ क्षेत्र-ईश्यै स्वाहा

Namaskar to the Mother, who in the female counterpart of the ruler of material existence.

343. ॐ क्षेत्रक्षेत्रज्ञपालिन्यै नमः
ॐ क्षेत्र-क्षेत्रज्ञ-पालिन्यै स्वाहा

Namaskar to the Mother, who is the protector of matter and the knower of matter.

344. ॐ क्षयवृद्धिविनिर्मुक्तायै नमः
ॐ क्षय-वृद्धि-विनिर्मुक्तायै स्वाहा

Namaskar to the Mother, who is free from decay and growth.

345. ॐ क्षेत्रपालसमर्चितायै नमः
ॐ क्षेत्रपाल-समर्चितायै स्वाहा

Namaskar to the Mother, who is properly worshipped by the Kshetrapala – a child incarnation of Shiva.

346. ॐ विजयायै नमः
ॐ विजयायै स्वाहा

Namaskar to the Ever victorious Mother.

347. ॐ विमलायै नमः
ॐ विमलायै स्वाहा

Namaskar to the Immaculate Mother.

348. ॐ वन्द्यायै नमः
ॐ वन्द्यायै स्वाहा

Namaskar to the Adorable Mother.

349. ॐ वन्दारुजनवत्सलायै नमः
ॐ वन्दारु-जन-वत्सलायै स्वाहा

Namaskar to the Yearning Mother, who protects and nourishes those, who worship her with adoration.

350. ॐ वाग्वादिन्यै नमः
ॐ वाक्-वादिन्यै स्वाहा

Namaskar to the Mother, who is the Speaker of 'Vak' – speech on the tongue of all her devotees.

351. ॐ वामकेश्यै नमः
ॐ वाम-केश्यै स्वाहा

Namaskar to the Mother with Beautiful hair.

352. ॐ वह्निमण्डलवासिन्यै नमः
ॐ वह्नि-मण्डल-वासिन्यै स्वाहा

Namaskar to the Mother abiding in the circle of fire.

353. ॐ भक्तिमत्कल्पलतिकायै नमः
ॐ भक्तिमत्-कल्प-लतिकायै स्वाहा

Namaskar to the Mother, who is Kalpa-Latika–wish-fulfilling creeper for the devotees.

354. ॐ पशुपाशविमोचन्यै नमः
ॐ पशु-पाश-विमोचन्यै स्वाहा

Namaskar to the Mother, who releases the 'pashu' ignorant from 'pasha' – bondage.

355. ॐ संहृताशेषपाषण्डायै नमः
ॐ संहृताशेष-पाषण्डायै स्वाहा

Namaskar to the Mother – the destroyer of all heretics and illusion

356. ॐ सदाचारप्रवर्तिकायै नमः
ॐ सदाचार-प्रवर्तिकायै स्वाहा

Namaskar to the Mother, who incites to right action.

357. ॐ तापत्रयाग्निसन्तप्तसमाह्लादनचन्द्रिकायै नमः
ॐ ताप-त्रय-अग्नि-सन्तप्त-समाह्लादन-चन्द्रिकायै स्वाहा

Namaskar to the Mother, having the moonlight delighting, tormented by the fire of triple fire.

358. ॐ तरुण्यै नमः
ॐ तरुण्यै स्वाहा

Namaskar to the Ever young Mother.

359. ॐ तापसाराध्यायै नमः
ॐ तापसाराध्यायै स्वाहा

Namaskar to the Mother, who is worshipped by ascetics.

360. ॐ तनुमध्यायै नमः
ॐ तनु-मध्यायै स्वाहा

Namaskar to the Slender-waisted Mother.

361. ॐ तमोपहायै नमः
ॐ तमोपहायै स्वाहा

Namaskar to the Mother–the remover of darkness.

362. ॐ चित्यै नमः
ॐ चित्यै स्वाहा

Namaskar to the Mother, who is 'Chitti' – the Supramental Consciousness.

363. ॐ तत्पदलक्ष्यार्थायै नमः
ॐ तत्-पद-लक्ष्यार्थायै स्वाहा

Namaskar to the Mother, who is denoted by the term 'Tad' – 'conditioned that'.

364. ॐ चिदेकरसरूपिण्यै नमः
ॐ चित-एक-रस-रूपिण्यै स्वाहा

Namaskar to the Mother with one essence of Intelligence.

365. ॐ स्वात्मानन्दलवीभूतब्रह्माद्यानन्दसन्तत्यै नमः
ॐ स्वात्मानन्द-लवी-भूत-ब्रह्म-आद्यानन्द-सन्तत्यै स्वाहा

Namaskar to the Mother, whose own nature is Supreme bliss, and the totality of the bliss of Brahma, etc., is but a minute one.

366. ॐ परायै नमः
ॐ परायै स्वाहा

Namaskar to the Para – Supreme Mother.

367. ॐ प्रत्यक्चितीरूपायै नमः
ॐ प्रत्यक्-चिती-रूपायै स्वाहा

Namaskar to the Mother in the form of Consciousness turning inward as the unmanifest Reality.

368. ॐ पश्यन्त्यै नमः
ॐ पश्यन्त्यै स्वाहा

Namaskar to the Pashyanti Mother – above the path of action.

369. ॐ परदेवतायै नमः
ॐ पर-देवतायै स्वाहा

Namaskar to the Mother as Supreme Deity of universe.

370. ॐ मध्यमायै नमः
ॐ मध्यमायै स्वाहा

Namaskar to the Mother Madhyama–neither 'Pashyanti' nor 'Vaikhari', but the midst one.

371. ॐ वैखरीरूपायै नमः
ॐ वैखरी-रूपायै स्वाहा

Namaskar to the Vaikhari Mother – speech in the physical form.

372. ॐ भक्तमानसहंसिकायै नमः
ॐ भक्त-मानस-हंसिकायै स्वाहा

Namaskar to the Mother, who is swan in the minds of the devotees.

373. ॐ कामेश्वरप्राणनाड्यै नमः
ॐ कामेश्वर-प्राण-नाड्यै स्वाहा

Namaskar to the Mother, who is the vital force and pulse beats of Kameshvara – the Lord of universe.

374. ॐ कृतज्ञायै नमः
ॐ कृतज्ञायै स्वाहा

Namaskar to the Mother, who judges actions.

375. ॐ कामपूजितायै नमः
ॐ काम-पूजितायै स्वाहा

Namaskar to the Mother, who is adored by Kama – god of Love.

376. ॐ श्रृङ्गाररससम्पूर्णायै नमः
ॐ श्रृङ्गार-रस-सम्पूर्णायै स्वाहा

Namaskar to the Mother, who is filled with the perfection of sentimental love.

377. ॐ जयायै नमः
ॐ जयायै स्वाहा

Namaskar to the Victorious Mother.

378. ॐ जालन्धरस्थितायै नमः
ॐ जालन्धर-स्थितायै स्वाहा

Namaskar to the Mother, who remains in the Jalandhara pitham.

379. ॐ ओड्याणपीठनिलयायै नमः
ॐ ओड्याण-पीठ-निलयायै स्वाहा

Namaskar to the Mother, who abides in the seat of 'Odhyana' – a Shakti pitham.

380. ॐ बिन्दुमण्डलवासिन्यै नमः
ॐ बिन्दु-मण्डल-वासिन्यै स्वाहा

Namaskar to the Mother, who dwells in the 'Bindu-mandala' – white circle of pure consciousness.

381. ॐ रहोयागक्रमाराध्यायै नमः
ॐ रहो-याग-क्रम-आराध्यायै स्वाहा

Namaskar to the Mother, who is secretly worshipped by sacrificial practices.

382. ॐ रहस्तर्पणतर्पितायै नमः
ॐ रहस्-तर्पण-तर्पितायै स्वाहा

Namaskar to the Mother, who is pleased by the secret oblations.

383. ॐ सद्यःप्रसादिन्यै नमः
ॐ सद्यः प्रसादिन्यै स्वाहा

Namaskar to the Mother, who confers immediate grace.

384. ॐ विश्वसाक्षिण्यै नमः
ॐ विश्व-साक्षिण्यै स्वाहा

Namaskar to the Mother as being the witness of the universe.

385. ॐ साक्षिवर्जितायै नमः
ॐ साक्षि-वर्जितायै स्वाहा

Namaskar to the Mother, who is witnessed by none.

386. ॐ षडड़गदेवतायुक्तायै नमः
ॐ षडङ्ग-देवता-युक्तायै स्वाहा

Namaskar to the Mother, who is accompanied by the deities of six limbs.

387. ॐ षाड्गुण्यपरिपूरितायै नमः
ॐ षाड्गुण्य-परि-पूरितायै स्वाहा

Namaskar to the Mother, who is all perfection of the six qualities.

388. ॐ नित्यक्लिन्नायै नमः
ॐ नित्य-क्लिन्नायै स्वाहा

Namaskar to the Ever compassionate Mother.

389. ॐ निरुपमायै नमः
ॐ निरुपमायै स्वाहा

Namaskar to the Mother, who has no similie – an equal.

390. ॐ निर्वाणसुखदायिन्यै नमः
ॐ निर्वाण-सुख-दायिन्यै नमः

Namaskar to the Mother, who grants the joy of 'Nirvana' – final beautitude.

391. ॐ नित्याषोडशिकारूपायै नमः
ॐ नित्या-षोडशिका-रूपायै स्वाहा

Namaskar to the Mother in the form of sixteen eternal deities.

392. ॐ श्रीकण्ठार्धशरीरिण्यै नमः
ॐ श्रीकण्ठ-अर्धशरीरिण्यै स्वाहा

Namaskar to the Mother, who posseses half the body of Srikantha – the throat with poison of Shiva.

393. ॐ प्रभावत्यै नमः
ॐ प्रभावत्यै स्वाहा

Namaskar to the Luminous Mother.

394. ॐ प्रभारूपायै नमः
ॐ प्रभा-रूपायै स्वाहा

Namaskar to the Mother in the form of effulgence.

395. ॐ प्रसिद्धायै नमः
ॐ प्रसिद्धायै स्वाहा

Namaskar to the Celebrated Mother.

396. ॐ परमेश्वर्यै नमः
ॐ परमेश्वर्यै स्वाहा

Namaskar to the Mother as Supreme ruler.

397. ॐ मूलप्रकृत्यै नमः
ॐ मूल-प्रकृत्यै स्वाहा

Namaskar to the Mother of Primal Prakriti.

398. ॐ अव्यक्तायै नमः
ॐ अव्यक्तायै स्वाहा

Namaskar to the Mother present in the undeveloped creation.

399. ॐ व्यक्ताव्यक्तस्वरूपिण्यै नमः
ॐ व्यक्त-अव्यक्त-स्वरूपिण्यै स्वाहा

Namaskar to the Mother in her own form of manifestation and unmanifestation.

400. ॐ व्यापिन्यै नमः
ॐ व्यापिन्यै स्वाहा

Namaskar to the All-pervading Mother.

401. ॐ विविधाकारायै नमः
ॐ विविध-आकारायै स्वाहा

Namaskar to the Mother, who is of multiform.

402. ॐ विद्याविद्यास्वरूपिण्यै नमः
ॐ विद्या-विद्यास्वरूपिण्यै स्वाहा

Namaskar to the Mother in the form of knowledge and ignorance.

403. ॐ महाकामेशनयनकुमदाह्लादकौमुद्यै नमः
ॐ महा-कामेश-नयन-कुमुद-आह्लाद-कौमुद्यै स्वाहा

Namaskar to the Mother with the moonlight which gladdens the 'Kumud' flowers of the eyes of Maha Kamesha – the Supreme Lord.

404. ॐ भक्तहार्दतमोभेदभानुमद्भानुसन्तत्यै नमः
ॐ भक्त-हार्द-तमो-भेद-भानुमद्-भानुसन्तत्यै स्वाहा

Namaskar to the Mother in the form of sunbeam which dispells darkness from the heart of her devotees.

405. ॐ शिवदूत्यै नमः
ॐ शिव-दूत्यै स्वाहा

Namaskar to the Shiva-dooti Mother – having Shiva as her messenger.

406. ॐ शिवाराध्यायै नमः
ॐ शिव-आराध्यायै स्वाहा

Namaskar to the Mother, who is worshipped by Shiva.

407. ॐ शिवमूर्त्यै नमः
ॐ शिव-मूर्त्यै स्वाहा

Namaskar to the Mother, who is in the form of Shiva.

408. ॐ शिवङ्कर्यै नमः
ॐ शिवङ्-कर्यै स्वाहा

Namaskar to the Mother – the giver of happiness.

409. ॐ शिवप्रियायै नमः
ॐ शिव-प्रियायै स्वाहा

Namaskar to the Mother – the beloved of Shiva.

410. ॐ शिवपरायै नमः
ॐ शिव-परायै स्वाहा

Namaskar to the Mother, who is beyond Shiva.

411. ॐ शिष्टेष्टायै नमः
ॐ शिष्ट-इष्टायै स्वाहा

Namaskar to the Mother as desired by the wise.

412. ॐ शिष्टपूजितायै नमः
ॐ शिष्ट-पूजितायै स्वाहा

Namaskar to the Mother, who is worshipped by Shishtas – recipient of the Vedic knowledge.

413. ॐ अप्रमेयायै नमः
ॐ अप्रमेयायै स्वाहा

Namaskar to the Immeasurable Mother.

414. ॐ स्वप्रकाशाय नमः
ॐ स्वप्रकाशाय स्वाहा

Namaskar to the Self-effulgent Mother.

415. ॐ मनोवाचामगोचरायै नमः
ॐ मनो-वाचाम्-अगोचरायै स्वाहा

Namaskar to the Mother, who is beyond mind and speech.

416. ॐ चिच्छकत्यै नमः
ॐ चित्-शक्तये स्वाहा

Namaskar to the Mother, who is the power of Consciousness.

417. ॐ चेतनारूपायै नमः
ॐ चेतना-रूपायै स्वाहा

Namaskar to the Mother, who is in the nature of pure-intelligence.

418. ॐ जडशक्त्यै नमः
ॐ जड-शक्तये स्वाहा

Namaskar to the Mother, having the dormant energy.

419. ॐ जडात्मिकायै नमः
ॐ जड-आत्मिकायै स्वाहा

Namaskar to the Mother, who is the Objective-world.

420. ॐ गायत्र्यै नमः
ॐ गायत्र्यै स्वाहा

Namaskar to the Mother Gayatri.

421. ॐ व्याहृत्यै नमः
ॐ व्याहृत्यै स्वाहा

Namaskar to the Mother Vyahrati – the Utterance.

422. ॐ सन्ध्यायै नमः
ॐ सन्ध्यायै स्वाहा

Namaskar to the Mother Sandhya – the junction.

423. ॐ द्विजवृन्दनिषेवितायै नमः
ॐ द्विज-वृन्द-निषेवितायै स्वाहा

Namaskar to the Mother, who is worshipped by the twice-born initiated persons.

424. ॐ तत्वासनायै नमः
ॐ तत्व-आसनायै स्वाहा

Namaskar to the Mother, who is having the categories as her seat.

425. ॐ तस्मै नमः
ॐ तस्मै स्वाहा

Namaskar to 'That' Mother.

426. ॐ तुभ्यं नमः
ॐ तुभ्यं स्वाहा

Namaskar to 'Thou' Mother.

427. ॐ अय्यै नमः
ॐ अय्यै स्वाहा

Namaskar to 'O Sweet Mother'

428. ॐ पञ्चकोशान्तरस्थितायै नमः
ॐ पञ्च-कोशान्तर-स्थितायै स्वाहा

Namaskar to the Mother, who resides in the five-sheaths.

429. ॐ निःसीममहिम्ने नमः
ॐ निसीम-महिम्ने स्वाहा

Namaskar to the Mother, who has no boundary.

430. ॐ नित्ययौवनायै नमः
ॐ नित्य-यौवनायै स्वाहा

Namaskar to the Ever young Mother.

431. ॐ मदशालिन्यै नमः
ॐ मद-शालिन्यै स्वाहा

Namaskar to the Mother, who is the Radiant uncontaminated bliss.

432. ॐ मदघूर्णितरक्ताक्ष्यै नमः
ॐ मद-घूर्णित-रक्त-अक्ष्यै स्वाहा

Namaskar to the Mother, having red eyes rolled with rapture.

433. ॐ मदपाटलगण्डभुवे नमः
ॐ मद-पाटल-गण्ड-भुवे स्वाहा

Namaskar to the Mother having cheeks blushed with rapture.

434. ॐ चन्दनद्रवादिग्धाङ्गयै नमः
ॐ चन्दन-द्रव-दिग्ध-अङ्गयै स्वाहा

Namaskar to the Mother, whose body is smeared with 'sandal' paste.

435. ॐ चाम्पेयकुसुमप्रियायै नमः
ॐ चाम्पेय-कुसुम-प्रियायै स्वाहा

Namaskar to the Mother, who is fond of a 'Champaka' flower.

436. ॐ कुशलायै नमः
ॐ कुशलायै स्वाहा

Namaskar to the Skilful Mother.

437. ॐ कोमलाकारायै नमः
ॐ कोमल-आकारायै स्वाहा

Namaskar.to the Mother, whose formation is tender and graceful.

438. ॐ कुरुकुल्लायै नमः
ॐ कुरु-कुल्लायै स्वाहा

Namaskar to the Mother Kurukulla.

439. ॐ कुलेश्वर्यै नमः
ॐ कुल-ईश्वर्यै स्वाहा

Namaskar to the Kuleshwari Mother – the presiding force of 'Triad' of the Trika System.

440. ॐ कुलकुण्डालयायै नमः
ॐ कुल-कुण्डालयायै स्वाहा

Namaskar to the Mother, who abides in the Kulakunda – the centre of the 'Muladhara'.

441. ॐ कौलमार्गतत्परसेवितायै नमः
ॐ कौल-मार्ग-तत्पर-सेवितायै स्वाहा

Namaskar to the Mother, who is worshipped by those, devoted to the Kula-path.

442. ॐ कुमारगणनाथाम्बायै नमः
ॐ कुमार-गणनाथ-अम्बायै स्वाहा

Namaskar to the Mother of Kumar-Skanda and Gananatha - Ganesha.

443. ॐ तुष्टयै नमः
ॐ तुष्टयै स्वाहा

Namaskar to the Mother present in Contentment.

444. ॐ पुष्टयै नमः
ॐ पुष्टयै स्वाहा

Namaskar to the Mother in the form of Nourishment.

445. ॐ मत्यै नमः
ॐ मत्यै स्वाहा

Namaskar to the Intelligent Mother.

446. ॐ धृत्यै नमः
ॐ धृत्यै स्वाहा

Namaskar to the Determined Mother.

447. ॐ शान्त्यै नमः
ॐ शान्त्यै स्वाहा

Namaskar to the Tranquil Mother.

448. ॐ स्वस्तिमत्यै नमः
ॐ स्वस्तिमत्यै स्वाहा

Namaskar to the Ever Real Mother.

449. ॐ कान्त्यै नमः
ॐ कान्त्यै स्वाहा

Namaskar to the Effulgent Mother.

450. ॐ नन्दिन्यै नमः
ॐ नन्दिन्यै स्वाहा

Namaskar to the Mother – the daughter of Nanda–Kamadhenu.

451. ॐ विघ्ननाशिन्यै नमः
ॐ विघ्न-नाशिन्यै स्वाहा

Namaskar to the Mother, who is the destroyer of obstacles.

452. ॐ तेजोवत्यै नमः
ॐ तेजोवत्यै स्वाहा

Namaskar to the Splendourous Mother.

453. ॐ त्रिनयनायै नमः
ॐ त्रि-नयनायै स्वाहा

Namaskar to the Three-eyed Mother.

454. ॐ लोलाक्षीकामरूपिण्यै नमः
ॐ लोलाक्षी-काम-रूपिण्यै स्वाहा

Namaskar to the Mother, who is in the form of the desire Yogeshvari.

455. ॐ मालिन्यै नमः
ॐ मालिन्यै स्वाहा

Namaskar to the Garland wearing Mother.

456. ॐ हंसिन्यै नमः
ॐ हंसिन्यै स्वाहा

Namaskar to the 'Swan Mother.'

457. ॐ मात्रे नमः
ॐ मात्रे स्वाहा

Namaskar to the Mother Matrika.

458. ॐ मलयाचलवासिन्यै नमः
ॐ मलयाचल-वासिन्यै स्वाहा

Namaskar to the Mother, who has her residence in the Malaya-mountains.

459. ॐ सुमुख्यै नमः
ॐ सुमुख्यै स्वाहा

Namaskar to the 'Lovely-faced Mother.'

460. ॐ नलिन्यै नमः
ॐ नलिन्यै स्वाहा

Namaskar to the 'Lotus Mother'.

461. ॐ सुभ्रवे नमः
ॐ सुभ्रवे स्वाहा

Namaskar to the Mother, as having beautiful eye-brows.

462. ॐ शोभनायै नमः
ॐ शोभनायै स्वाहा

Namaskar to the Graceful Mother.

463. ॐ सुरनायिकायै नमः
ॐ सुर-नायिकायै स्वाहा

Namaskar to the Mother, who is the leader of the Devas – brigh one's.

464. ॐ काल-कण्ठयै नमः
ॐ काल-कण्ठयै स्वाहा

Namaskar to the Mother Kalakantha having soft-throat.

465. ॐ कान्तिमत्यै नमः
ॐ कान्ति-मत्यै स्वाहा

Namaskar to the Radiant Mother.

466. ॐ क्षोभिण्यै नमः
ॐ क्षोभिण्यै स्वाहा

Namaskar to the 'Exciting Mother'.

467. ॐ सूक्ष्मरूपिण्यै नमः
ॐ सूक्ष्म-रूपिण्यै स्वाहा

Namaskar to the Mother having subtle form.

468. ॐ वज्रेश्वर्यै नमः
ॐ वज्र-ईश्वर्यै स्वाहा

Namaskar to the Vajreshvari Mother–the tutelary deity of the Jalandhara Pitham.

469. ॐ वामदेव्यै नमः
ॐ वाम-देव्यै स्वाहा

Namaskar to the Mother, as the wife of Vamadeva.

470. ॐ वयोऽवस्थाविवर्जितायै नमः
ॐ वयोऽवस्था-विवर्जितायै स्वाहा

Namaskar to the Mother, who is devoid of the different stages of life.

471. ॐ सिद्धेश्वर्यै नमः
ॐ सिद्ध-ईश्वर्यै स्वाहा

Namaskar to the Mother, who is the Queen of the Siddhas – the perfect one's.

472. ॐ सिद्धविद्यायै नमः
ॐ सिद्ध-विद्यायै स्वाहा

Namaskar to the Mother, who has perfect knowledge.

473. ॐ सिद्धमात्रे नमः
ॐ सिद्ध-मात्रे स्वाहा

Namaskar to the Mother, as being the Mother of the Siddhas.

474. ॐ यशस्विन्यै नमः
ॐ यशस्विन्यै स्वाहा

Namaskar to the Famous Mother.

475. ॐ विशुद्धिचक्रनिलयायै नमः
ॐ विशुद्धि-चक्र-निलयायै स्वाहा

Namaskar to the Mother, who abides in the Vishudhi Chakra – the region at the base of the throat.

476. ॐ आरक्तवर्णायै नमः
ॐ आरक्त-वर्णायै स्वाहा

Namaskar to the Rosy-Complexioned Mother.

477. ॐ त्रिलोचनायै नमः
ॐ त्रि-लोचनायै स्वाहा

Namaskar to the Three-eyed Mother.

478. ॐ खट्वाङ्गादिप्रहरणायै नमः
ॐ खट्वाङ्ग-आदि-प्रहरणायै स्वाहा

Namaskar to the Mother, as holding the foot of a cot as a weapon.

479. ॐ वदनैकसमन्वितायै नमः
ॐ वदन-एक-समन्वितायै स्वाहा

Namaskar to the Mother, as possessing one face.

480. ॐ पायसान्नप्रियायै नमः
ॐ पायस-अन्न-प्रियायै स्वाहा

Namaskar to the Mother, who is fond of milk preparation.

481. ॐ त्वकस्थायै नमः
ॐ त्वकस्थायै स्वाहा

Namaskar to the Mother, who abides in the organ of touch.

482. ॐ पशुलोकभयङ्कर्यै नमः
ॐ पशु-लोक-भयङ्कर्यै स्वाहा

Namaskar to the Mother, who fills the ignorant with fear.

483. ॐ अमृतादिमहाशक्तिसंवृतायै नमः
ॐ अमृत-आदि-महा-शक्ति-संवृतायै स्वाहा

Namaskar to the Mother, surrounded by the Amrita and other Shaktis – powers.

484. ॐ डाकिनीश्वर्यै नमः
ॐ डाकिनी-ईश्वर्यै स्वाहा

Namaskar to the Mother, who is the Ruler Dakini.

485. ॐ अनाहताब्जनिलयायै नमः
ॐ अनाहत-अब्ज-निलयायै स्वाहा

Namaskar to the Mother, who abides in the Anahat-lotus – the heart region.

486. ॐ श्यामाभायै नमः
ॐ श्यामा-आभायै स्वाहा

Namaskar to the Mother, who is Dark in hue.

487. ॐ वदनद्वयायै नमः
ॐ वदन-द्वयायै स्वाहा

Namaskar to the Two-faced Mother.

488. ॐ दंष्ट्रोज्ज्वलायै नमः
ॐ दंष्ट्रोज्ज्वलायै स्वाहा

Namaskar to the Mother, who is with Shining tusks.

489. ॐ अक्षमालादिधरायै नमः
ॐ अक्ष-माला-आदि-धरायै स्वाहा

Namaskar to the Mother, as wearing the garland of Aksha beads etc.

490. ॐ रुधिरसंस्थितायै नमः
ॐ रुधिर-संस्थितायै स्वाहा

Namaskar to the Mother, who resides in the blood cells.

491. ॐ कालरात्र्यादिशक्तयौघवृतायै नमः
ॐ कालरात्रि-आदिशक्ति-उघवृतायै स्वाहा

Namaskar to the Mother, attended by host of Shaktis – Kalaratri etc.

492. ॐ स्निग्धौदनप्रियायै नमः
ॐ स्निग्ध-उदन-प्रियायै स्वाहा

Namaskar to the Mother fond of greasy food.

493. ॐ राकिण्यम्बास्वरूपिण्यै नमः
ॐ राकिनी-अम्बा-स्वरूपिण्यै स्वाहा

Namaskar to the Mother, who grants boons to Mahavira and Indra.

494. ॐ महावीरेन्द्रवरदायै नमः
ॐ महा-वीरेन्द्र-वरदायै स्वाहा

Namaskar to the Mother, assuming the form of Rakini – Amba.

495. ॐ मणिपूराब्जनिलयायै नमः
ॐ मणिपूर-अब्ज-निलयायै स्वाहा

Namaskar to the Mother, who abides in the Manipura lotus – naval region.

496. ॐ वदनत्रयसंयुतायै नमः
ॐ वदन-त्रय-संयुतायै स्वाहा

Namaskar to the Mother, having three faces.

497. ॐ वज्रादिकायुधोपेतायै नमः
ॐ वज्र-आदि-कायुधोपेतायै स्वाहा

Namaskar to the Mother, who is armed with the thunderbolt and other weapons.

498. ॐ डामर्यादिभिरावृतायै नमः
ॐ डामर्य-आदिभि-आवृतायै स्वाहा

Namaskar to the Mother, attended by Damari etc. powers.

499. ॐ रक्तवर्णायै नमः
ॐ रक्त-वर्णायै स्वाहा

Namaskar to the Mother, having Blood colour.

500. ॐ मांसनिष्ठायै नमः
ॐ मांस-निष्ठायै स्वाहा

Namaskar to the Mother, presiding over flesh.

501. ॐ गुडान्नप्रीतीमानसायै नमः
ॐ गुड-अन्न-प्रीत-मानसायै स्वाहा

Namaskar to the Mother, who is fond of sweet food.

502. ॐ समस्तभक्तसुखदायै नमः
ॐ समस्त-भक्त-सुखदायै स्वाहा

Namaskar to the Mother, who is conferring happiness on all her devotees.

503. ॐ लाकिन्यम्बास्वरूपिण्यै नमः
ॐ लाकिनी-अम्बा-स्वरूपिण्यै स्वाहा

Namaskar to the Mother, assuming the form of the Mother Lakini.

504. ॐ स्वाधिष्ठानाम्बुजगतायै नमः
ॐ स्वाधिष्ठान-अम्बुज-गतायै स्वाहा

Namaskar to the Mother, who is residing in the Svadhisthan lotus – base of the procreation.

505. ॐ चतुर्वक्त्रमनोहरायै नमः
ॐ चतुर्वक्त्र-मनोहरायै स्वाहा

Namaskar to the Fascinating four-faced Mother.

506. ॐ शूलाद्यायुधसम्पन्नायै नमः
ॐ शूल-आदि-आयुध-सम्पन्नायै स्वाहा

Namaskar to the Mother, who is armed with the trident and other weapons.

507. ॐ पीतवर्णायै नमः
ॐ पीत-वर्णायै स्वाहा

Namaskar to the Yellow hued Mother.

508. ॐ अतिगर्वितायै नमः
ॐ अति-गर्वितायै स्वाहा

Namaskar to the Very Proud Mother.

509. ॐ मेदोनिष्ठायै नमः
ॐ मेदो-निष्ठायै स्वाहा

Namaskar to the Mother, presiding over fat.

510. ॐ मधुप्रीतायै नमः
ॐ मधुप्रीतायै स्वाहा

Namaskar to the Mother, who likes offering of honey.

511. ॐ बन्धिन्यादिसमन्वितायै नमः
ॐ बन्धिन्यादि-समन्वितायै स्वाहा

Namaskar to the Mother, who is attended by Bandhani and other deities.

512. ॐ दध्यन्नासक्तहृदयायै नमः
ॐ दध्यन्नासक्त-हृदयायै स्वाहा

Namaskar to the Mother, who is fond of food mixed with curd.

513. ॐ काकिनीरूपधारिण्यै नमः
ॐ काकिनी-रूप-धारिण्यै स्वाहा

Namaskar to the Mother, who is assuming the form of Kakini.

514. ॐ मूलाधाराम्बुजारूढायै नमः
ॐ मूलाधार-अम्बुज-आरूढायै स्वाहा

Namaskar to the Mother, who ascends the Muladhara lotus.

515. ॐ पञ्चवक्त्रायै नमः
ॐ पञ्च-वक्त्रायै स्वाहा

Namaskar to the Five-faced Mother.

516. ॐ अस्थिसंस्थितायै नमः
ॐ अस्थि-संस्थितायै स्वाहा

Namaskar to the Mother, who presides over the bones.

517. ॐ अङ्.कुशादिप्रहरणायै नमः
ॐ अङ्.कुश-आदि-प्रहरणायै स्वाहा

Namaskar to the Mother, who is armed with the elephant hook etc.

518. ॐ वरदादिनिषेवितायै नमः
ॐ वरद-आदि-निषेवितायै स्वाहा

Namaskar to the Mother, who is attended by Varada and other Shaktis.

519. ॐ मुद्गौदनासक्तचित्तायै नमः
ॐ मुद्गौदन-आसक्त-चित्तायै स्वाहा

Namaskar to the Mother, who is fond of food mixed with pulse.

520. ॐ साकिन्यम्बास्वरूपिण्यै नमः
ॐ साकिनी-अम्बा-स्वरूपिण्यै स्वाहा

Namaskar to the Mother, who assumes the form of Sakini Amba.

521. ॐ आज्ञाचक्राब्जनिलयायै नमः
ॐ आज्ञा-चक्र-अब्ज-निलयायै स्वाहा

Namaskar to the Mother, who resides over the Ajna lotus location – between two eyebrows.

522. ॐ शुक्लवर्णायै नमः
ॐ शुक्ल-वर्णायै स्वाहा

Namaskar to the White hued Mother.

523. ॐ षडाननायै नमः
ॐ षडाननायै स्वाहा

Namaskar to the Six-faced Mother.

524. ॐ मज्जासंस्थायै नमः
ॐ मज्जा-संस्थायै स्वाहा

Namaskar to the Mother, presiding over the marrow.

525. ॐ हंसवतीमुख्यशक्तिसमन्वितायै नमः
ॐ हंसवती-मुख्य-शक्ति-समन्वितायै स्वाहा

Namaskar to the Mother, who is attended by Hamsavati and other Shaktis.

526. ॐ हरिद्रान्नैकरसिकायै नमः
ॐ हरिद्रान्न-एक-रसिकायै स्वाहा

Namaskar to the Mother, who is fond of safron flavoured food.

527. ॐ हाकिनीरूपधारिण्यै नमः
ॐ हाकिनी-रूप-धारिण्यै स्वाहा

Namaskar to the Mother assuming the form of Hakini.

528. ॐ सहस्रदलपद्मस्थायै नमः

ॐ सहस्र-दल-पद्मस्थायै स्वाहा

Namaskar to the Mother residing in the thousand-petalled lotus – located in the skull.

529. ॐ सर्ववर्णोपशोभितायै नमः

ॐ सर्व-वर्णे-उपशोभितायै स्वाहा

Namaskar to the Brilliant Mother with all colours.

530. ॐ सर्वायुधधरायै नमः

ॐ सर्व-आयुध-धरायै स्वाहा

Namaskar to the Mother armed with all weapons.

531. ॐ शुक्लसंस्थितायै नमः

ॐ शुक्ल-संस्थितायै स्वाहा

Namaskar to the Mother, residing in the very essence of Semen.

532. ॐ सर्वतोमुख्यै नमः

ॐ सर्वतोमुख्यै स्वाहा

Namaskar to the Mother, facing on every side.

533. ॐ सर्वौदनप्रीतचित्तायै नमः

ॐ सर्वौदन-प्रीत-चित्तायै स्वाहा

Namaskar to the Mother, who is fond of all kinds of food.

534. ॐ याकिन्यम्बास्वरूपिण्यै नमः

ॐ याकिनी-अम्बा-स्वरूपिण्यै स्वाहा

Namaskar to the Mother, assuming the form of the Yakini Amba.

535. ॐ स्वाहायै नमः

ॐ स्वाहायै स्वाहा

Namaskar to the Mother Svaha – an utterance when the oblation is offered in the sacrificial fire.

536. ॐ स्वधायै नमः

ॐ स्वधायै स्वाहा

Namaskar to the Mother Svadha – an oblation offered to the deceased ancestors.

537. ॐ अमर्त्यै नमः
ॐ अमर्त्यै स्वाहा

Namaskar to the Mother devoid of intelligence–material existence.

538. ॐ मेधायै नमः
ॐ मेधायै स्वाहा

Namaskar to the Mother Intellect.

539. ॐ श्रुत्यै नमः
ॐ श्रुत्यै स्वाहा

Namaskar to the Mother Shruti – Veda Mata.

540. ॐ स्मृत्यै नमः
ॐ स्मृत्यै स्वाहा

Namaskar to the Mother Smriti – Recollection and code of conduct.

541. ॐ अनुत्तमायै नमः
ॐ अनुत्तमायै स्वाहा

Namaskar to the Best and Superior Mother.

542. ॐ पुण्यकीर्त्यै नमः
ॐ पुण्य-कीर्त्यै स्वाहा

Namaskar to the Mother famed for righteousness.

543. ॐ पुण्यलभ्यायै नमः
ॐ पुण्य-लभ्यायै स्वाहा

Namaskar to the Mother, attained through righteousness.

544. ॐ पुण्यश्रवणकीर्तनायै नमः
ॐ पुर्ण्य-श्रवण-कीर्तनायै स्वाहा

Namaskar to the Mother, who is the personification of Punya Shravan – holy hearing and Kirtan – praising.

545. ॐ पुलोमजार्चितायै नमः
ॐ पुलोमज-अर्चितायै स्वाहा

Namaskar to the Mother, worshipped by Pulmoja – Indra's spouse.

546. ॐ बन्धमोचन्यै नमः
ॐ बन्ध-मोचन्यै स्वाहा

Namaskar to the Mother, who is the remover of bonds.

547. ॐ बर्बरालकायै नमः
ॐ बर्बर-अलकायै स्वाहा

Namaskar to the Curly-haired Mother.

548. ॐ विमर्शरूपिण्यै नमः
ॐ विमर्श-रूपिण्यै स्वाहा

Namaskar to the Mother, who is the personification of Vimarsha – reflection, speech.

549. ॐ विद्यायै नमः
ॐ विद्यायै स्वाहा

Namaskar to the Mother Vidya – Knowledge.

550. ॐ वियदादिजगत्प्रसुवे नमः
ॐ वियत्-आदि-जगत्-प्रसुवे स्वाहा

Namaskar to the Universal Mother, where ether, etc. exists.

551. ॐ सर्वव्याधिप्रशमन्यै नमः
ॐ सर्व-व्याधि-प्रशमन्यै स्वाहा

Namaskar to the Mother, who alleviates all diseases.

552. ॐ सर्वमृत्युनिवारिण्यै नमः
ॐ सर्व-मृत्यु-निवारिण्यै स्वाहा

Namaskar to the Mother, who dispells all death.

553. ॐ अग्रगण्यायै नमः
ॐ अग्र-गण्यायै स्वाहा

Namaskar to the Mother as the First one.

554. ॐ अचिन्त्यरूपायै नमः
ॐ अचिन्त्य-रूपायै स्वाहा

Namaskar to the Mother, who is of unthinkable form.

555. ॐ कलिकल्मषनाशिन्यै नमः
ॐ कलि-कल्मष-नाशिन्यै स्वाहा

Namaskar to the Mother the destroyer of sin in the Kali-age.

556. ॐ कात्यायन्यै नमः
ॐ कात्यायन्यै स्वाहा

Namaskar to the Mother Katyayani.

557. ॐ कालहन्त्र्यै नमः
ॐ काल-हन्त्र्यै स्वाहा

Namaskar to the Mother the destroyer of sin.

558. ॐ कमलाक्षनिषेवितायै नमः
ॐ कमलाक्ष-निषेवितायै स्वाहा

Namaskar to the Mother, who is worshipped by Kamalaksha – Vishnu having lotus-eyes.

559. ॐ ताम्बूलपूरितमुख्यै नमः
ॐ ताम्बूल-पूरित-मुख्यै स्वाहा

Namaskar to the Mother, whose mouth is filled with betel.

560. ॐ दाडिमीकुसुमप्रभायै नमः
ॐ दाडिमी-कुसुम-प्रभायै स्वाहा

Namaskar to the Mother, having the hue of pomegranate flowers.

561. ॐ मृगाक्ष्यै नमः
ॐ मृगाक्ष्यै स्वाहा

Namaskar to the Fawn-eyed Mother.

562. ॐ मोहिन्यै नमः
ॐ मोहिन्यै स्वाहा

Namaskar to the Enchanting Mother.

563. ॐ मुख्यायै नमः
ॐ मुख्यायै स्वाहा

Namaskar to the Mother as the Chief one.

564. ॐ मृडान्यै नमः
ॐ मृडान्यै स्वाहा

Namaskar to the Mother, as being the wife of Mrida–Parama Shiva.

565. ॐ मित्ररूपिण्यै नमः
ॐ मित्र-रूपिण्यै स्वाहा

Namaskar to the Mother as a Friend.

566. ॐ नित्यतृप्तायै नमः
ॐ नित्य-तृप्तायै स्वाहा

Namaskar to the Eternally-pleased Mother.

567. ॐ भक्तनिधये नमः
ॐ भक्त-निधये स्वाहा

Namaskar to the Mother, as being the Treasure of the devotees.

568. ॐ नियन्त्रयै नमः
ॐ नियन्त्रयै स्वाहा

Namaskar to the Mother being Supreme Controller.

569. ॐ निखिलेश्वेर्यै नमः
ॐ निखिल-ईश्वर्यै स्वाहा

Namaskar to the Mother, who is the Ruler of all.

570. ॐ मैत्र्यादिवासनालभ्यायै नमः
ॐ मैत्र्यादि-वासना-लभ्यायै स्वाहा

Namaskar to the Mother, who is attained by the cultivation of Maitri etc. – friendship, compassion, complacency and indifference.

571. ॐ महाप्रलयसाक्षिण्यै नमः
ॐ महा-प्रलय-साक्षिण्यै स्वाहा

Namaskar to the Mother, who is witness to the Great Dissolution.

572. ॐ परायै शक्तयै नमः
ॐ परायै-शक्तयै स्वाहा

Namaskar to the Mother as the Supreme energy.

573. ॐ परायै निष्ठायै नमः
ॐ परायै-निष्ठायै स्वाहा

Namaskar to the Mother, who is the Supreme end.

574. ॐ प्रज्ञानघनरूपिण्यै नमः
ॐ प्रज्ञान-घन-रूपिण्यै स्वाहा

Namaskar to the Mother, having the Concentrated knowledge.

575. ॐ माध्वीपानालसायै नमः
ॐ माध्वी-पान-आलसायै स्वाहा

Namaskar to the Mother, who has become Introvert by drinking wine.

576. ॐ मत्तायै नमः
ॐ मत्तायै स्वाहा

Namaskar to the Ego-conscious state of Mother.

577. ॐ मातृकावर्णरूपिण्यै नमः
ॐ मातृका-वर्ण-रूपिण्यै स्वाहा

Namaskar to the Mother in the form of Matrika-letter from A to Ksha, of the Varnamala.

578. ॐ महाकैलासनिलयायै नमः
ॐ महा-कैलास-निलयायै स्वाहा

Namaskar to the Mother, who resides in the great Kailas mount.

579. ॐ मृणालमृदुदोर्लतायै नमः
ॐ मृणाल-मृदु-दोर्लतायै स्वाहा

Namaskar to the Mother, whose creeper-like arms are soft as the lotus stem.

580. ॐ महनीनायै नमः
ॐ महनीनायै स्वाहा

Namaskar to the Illustrious Mother.

581. ॐ दयामूर्त्यै नमः
ॐ दया-मूर्त्यै स्वाहा

Namaskar to the Mother, who is the very self of Compassion.

582. ॐ महासाम्राज्यशालिन्यै नमः
ॐ महा-साम्राज्य-शालिन्यै स्वाहा

Namaskar to the Mother, who is Resplendent with wide dominion.

583. ॐ आत्मविद्यायै नमः
ॐ आत्म-विद्यायै स्वाहा

Namaskar to the Mother, who is Atmavidya – the Knowledge of Self.

584. ॐ महाविद्यायै नमः
ॐ महा-विद्यायै स्वाहा

Namaskar to the Mother, who is Mahavidya – the Exalted Knowledge.

585. ॐ श्रीविद्यायै नमः
ॐ श्री-विद्यायै स्वाहा

Namaskar to the Mother, who is Sri Vidya – the Supreme Knowledge.

586. ॐ कामसेवितायै नमः
ॐ काम-सेवितायै स्वाहा

Namaskar to the Mother, who is attended by Kama – the bodiless one (or god of love).

587. ॐ श्रीषोडशाक्षरीविद्यायै नमः
ॐ श्री-षोडशाक्षरी-विद्यायै स्वाहा

Namaskar to the Mother, who is herself the knowledge of Sri Shodashakshari – the Silteen syllabled formula of Sri Vidya.

588. ॐ त्रिकूटायै नमः
ॐ त्रि-कूटायै स्वाहा

Namaskar to the Three-peaked Mother of Vaghbhava and other kutas.

589. ॐ कामकोटिकायै नमः
ॐ काम-कोटिकायै स्वाहा

Namaskar to the Mother, as having the spirit of Kama.

590. ॐ कटाक्षकिङ्करीभूतकमलाकोटिसेवितायै नमः
ॐ कटाक्ष-किङ्करी-भूत-कमला-कोटि-सेवितायै स्वाहा

Namaskar to the Mother, who is attended by millions of Kamalas – the Devi of fortune subdued by her glances.

591. ॐ शिरः स्थितायै नमः
ॐ शिरः स्थितायै स्वाहा

Namaskar to the Mother, who resides in the head.

592. ॐ चन्द्रनिभायै नमः
ॐ चन्द्र-निभायै स्वाहा

Namaskar to the Moon-like Mother.

593. ॐ भालस्थायै नमः
ॐ भालस्थायै स्वाहा

Namaskar to the Mother, who resides in the forehead.

594. ॐ इन्द्रधनुष्प्रभायै नमः
ॐ इन्द्रधनुष्-प्रभायै स्वाहा

Namaskar to the Rainbow-hued Mother.

595. ॐ हृदयस्थायै नमः
ॐ हृदय-स्थायै स्वाहा

Namaskar to the Mother, who resides in the heart.

596. ॐ रविप्रख्यायै नमः
ॐ रवि-प्रख्यायै स्वाहा

Namaskar to the Mother, who resembles the sun.

597. ॐ त्रिकोणान्तरदीपिकायै नमः
ॐ त्रिकोणान्तर-दीपिकायै स्वाहा

Namaskar to the Mother, who resides as light in the triangle.

598. ॐ दाक्षायण्यै नमः
ॐ दाक्षायण्यै स्वाहा

Namaskar to the Mother, the Daughter of Daksha.

599. ॐ दैत्यहन्त्र्यै नमः
ॐ दैत्य-हन्त्र्यै स्वाहा

Namaskar to the Mother, who is the Slayer of Daitya – Bhandasura.

600. ॐ दक्षयज्ञविनाशिन्यै नमः
ॐ दक्ष-यज्ञ-विनाशिन्यै स्वाहा

Namaskar to the Mother, who is the Destroyer of the sacrifice of Daksha-Prajapati.

601. ॐ दरान्दोलितदीर्घस्थायै नमः
ॐ दरान्दोलित-दीर्घस्थायै स्वाहा

Namaskar to the Mother, moving slowly with large eyes.

602. ॐ दरहासोज्जवलन्मुख्यै नमः
ॐ दर-हासोज्जवलन्-मुख्यै स्वाहा

Namaskar to the Mother, whose face shines with smiles.

603. ॐ गुरुमूर्त्यै नमः
ॐ गुरु-मूर्त्यै स्वाहा

Namaskar to the Mother, who assumes the form of a teacher.

604. ॐ गुणनिधये नमः
ॐ गुण-निधये स्वाहा

Namaskar to the Mother, who is the treasure house of qualities.

605. ॐ गोमात्रे नमः
ॐ गो-मात्रे स्वाहा

Namaskar to the Mother of Kine.

606. ॐ गुहजन्मभुवे नमः
ॐ गुह-जन्म-भुवे स्वाहा

Namaskar to the Mother of Guha-Subrahmanya.

607. ॐ देवेश्यै नमः
ॐ देवेश्यै स्वाहा

Namaskar to the Mother, who is the Ruler of gods.

608. ॐ दण्डनीतिस्थायै नमः
ॐ दण्ड-नीतिस्थायै स्वाहा

Namaskar to the Mother, who dwells in justice.

609. ॐ दहराकाशरूपिण्यै नमः
ॐ दहराकाश-रूपिण्यै स्वाहा

Namaskar to the Mother, who is like the small space in the heart.

610. ॐ प्रतिपन्मुख्यराकान्तति थिमण्डलपूजितायै नमः
ॐ प्रतिपन्-मुख्य-राकान्त-तिथि-मण्डल-पूजितायै स्वाहा

Namaskar to the Mother, who is worshipped on the group of tithis from Pratipada to Purnima.

611. ॐ कलात्मिकायै नमः
ॐ कला-आत्मिकायै स्वाहा

Namaskar to the Mother in the form of Kala-the lunar digit.

612. ॐ कलानाथाय नमः
ॐ कला-नाथाय स्वाहा

Namaskar to the Ruling Mother Kala.

613. ॐ काव्यालापविनोदिन्यै नमः
ॐ काव्य-आलाप-विनोदिन्यै स्वाहा

Namaskar to the Mother, who is Sporting with the poetical speech.

614. ॐ सचामररमावाणीसव्यदक्षिणसेवितायै नमः
ॐ सचामर-रमा-वाणी-सव्य-दक्षिण-सेवितायै स्वाहा

Namaskar to the Mother, who is attended on either side by Lakshmi and Sarasvati bearing Chamaras.

615. ॐ आदिशक्त्यै नमः
ॐ आदि-शक्त्यै स्वाहा

Namaskar to the Primordial Mother of Energy.

616. ॐ अमेयायै नमः
ॐ अमेयायै स्वाहा

Namaskar to the Immeasurable Mother.

617. ॐ आत्मने नमः
ॐ आत्मने स्वाहा

Namaskar to the Mother-Self.

618. ॐ परमायै नमः
ॐ परमायै स्वाहा

Namaskar to the Supreme Mother.

619. ॐ पावनाकृतये नमः
ॐ पावन-आकृतये स्वाहा

Namaskar to the Mother of pure form.

620. ॐ अनेककोटिब्रह्माण्डजनन्यै नमः
ॐ अनेक-कोटि-ब्रह्माण्ड-जनन्यै स्वाहा

Namaskar to the Mother, who is the creator of many Crores of worlds.

621. ॐ दिव्यविग्रहायै नमः
ॐ दिव्य-विग्रहायै स्वाहा

Namaskar to the Divinely-shaped Mother.

622. ॐ क्लीङ्कार्यै नमः
ॐ क्लीं-कार्यै स्वाहा

Namaskar to the Mother, who is the creator of the syllable 'Klim.'

623. ॐ केवलायै नमः
ॐ केवलायै स्वाहा

Namaskar to the Absolute Mother.

624. ॐ गुह्यायै नमः
ॐ गुह्यायै स्वाहा

Namaskar to the Mother of secrecy.

625. ॐ कैवल्यपददायिन्यै नमः
ॐ कैवल्य-पद-दायिन्यै स्वाहा

Namaskar to the Mother, who is the bestower of the solitary abode.

626. ॐ त्रिपुरायै नमः
ॐ त्रि-पुरायै स्वाहा

Namaskar to the Tripura Mother.

627. ॐ त्रिजगद्वन्द्यायै नमः
ॐ त्रि-जगत्-वन्द्यायै स्वाहा

Namaskar to the Mother, who is adored by the three worlds.

628. ॐ त्रिमूर्त्यै नमः
ॐ त्रि-मूर्त्यै स्वाहा

Namaskar to the Mother Trimurti.

629. ॐ त्रिदशेश्वर्यै नमः
ॐ त्रिदशेश्वर्यै स्वाहा

Namaskar to the Mother Sovereign of the thirty Ganas of gods.

630. ॐ त्र्यक्षर्यै नमः
ॐ त्रि-अक्षर्यै स्वाहा

Namaskar to the Three syllabled Mother.

631. ॐ दिव्यगन्धाढ्यायै नमः
ॐ दिव्य-गन्धाढ्यायै स्वाहा

Namaskar to the Mother, who is endowned with the divine perfume.

632. ॐ सिन्दूरतिलकाञ्चितायै नमः
ॐ सिन्दूर-तिलकाञ्चितायै स्वाहा

Namaskar to the Mother, who is adorned with Vermilion mark on her forehead.

633. ॐ उमायै नमः
ॐ उमायै स्वाहा

Namaskar to the Mother Uma.

634. ॐ शैलेन्द्रतनयायै नमः
ॐ शैलेन्द्र-तनयायै स्वाहा

Namaskar to the Mother, who is the Daughter of the King of mountains.

635. ॐ गौर्यै नमः
ॐ गौर्यै स्वाहा

Namaskar to the Mother Gauri.

636. ॐ गन्धर्वसेवितायै नमः
ॐ गन्धर्व-सेवितायै स्वाहा

Namaskar to the Mother who is attended by the Gandharavas.

637. ॐ विश्वगर्भायै नमः
ॐ विश्व-गर्भायै स्वाहा

Namaskar to the Mother, who has the Universe in Her womb.

638. ॐ स्वर्णगर्भायै नमः
ॐ स्वर्ण-गर्भायै स्वाहा

Namaskar to the Mother, who has the Golden womb.

639. ॐ अवरदायै नमः
ॐ अवरदायै स्वाहा

Namaskar to the Mother, who does not bestow grace on the unholy persons.

640. ॐ वागधीश्वर्यै नमः
ॐ वाक्-अधीश्वर्यै स्वाहा

Namaskar to the Mother, who is the Ruler of Speech.

641. ॐ ध्यानगम्यायै नमः
ॐ ध्यान-गम्यायै स्वाहा

Namaskar to the Mother, who can be attained by meditation.

642. ॐ अपरिच्छेदायै नमः
ॐ अपरि-च्छेदायै स्वाहा

Namaskar to the Unlimited Mother.

643. ॐ ज्ञानदायै नमः
ॐ ज्ञानदायै स्वाहा

Namaskar to the Mother, who grants knowledge.

644. ॐ ज्ञानविग्रहायै नमः
ॐ ज्ञान-विग्रहायै स्वाहा

Namaskar to the Mother, whose body is knowledge.

645. ॐ सर्ववेदान्तसंवेद्यायै नमः
ॐ सर्व-वेदान्त-संवेद्यायै स्वाहा

Namaskar to the Mother, who can be known through all the processes of Vedanta.

646. ॐ सत्यानन्दस्वरूपिण्यै नमः
ॐ सत्य-आनन्द-स्वरूपिण्यै स्वाहा

Namaskar to the Mother, who is of the form of existence and bliss.

647. ॐ लोपामुद्रार्चितायै नमः
ॐ लोपामुद्रा-अर्चितायै स्वाहा

Namaskar to the Mother, who is worshipped by Lopamudra.

648. ॐ लीलाक्लृप्तब्रगह्माण्डमण्डलायै नमः
ॐ लीला-क्लृप्त-ब्रह्माण्ड-मण्डलायै स्वाहा

Namaskar to the Mother, who formed the world systems as it were in her sport.

649. ॐ अदृश्यायै नमः
ॐ अदृश्यायै स्वाहा

Namaskar to the invisible Mother.

650. ॐ दृश्यरहितायै नमः
ॐ दृश्यरहितायै स्वाहा

Namaskar to the Mother, who has no empirical form.

651. ॐ विज्ञात्र्यै नमः
ॐ विज्ञात्र्यै स्वाहा

Namaskar to the Perceptive Mother.

652. ॐ वेद्यवर्जितायै नमः
ॐ वेद्य-वर्जितायै स्वाहा

Namaskar to the Mother, who Transcends the knowable.

653. ॐ योगिन्यै नमः
ॐ योगिन्यै स्वाहा

Namaskar to the Yogini Mother.

654. ॐ योगदायै नमः
ॐ योगदायै स्वाहा

Namaskar to the Mother, who is the Bestower of Yoga.

655. ॐ योग्यायै नमः
ॐ योग्यायै स्वाहा

Namaskar to the Supremely suitable Mother.

656. ॐ योगानन्दायै नमः
ॐ योगानन्दायै स्वाहा

Namaskar to the Mother, who is the Bliss of Yoga.

657. ॐ युगन्धरायै नमः
ॐ युगन्धरायै स्वाहा

Namaskar to the Mother, who is the Bearer of the Yoke.

658. ॐ इच्छाशक्तिज्ञानशक्तिक्रियाशक्तिस्वरूपिण्यै नमः
ॐ इच्छाशक्ति-ज्ञानशक्ति-क्रियाशक्ति-स्वरूपिण्यै स्वाहा

Namaskar to the Mother, who is the very nature of will power, wisdom power and the action power.

659. ॐ सर्वाधारायै नमः
ॐ सर्व-आधारायै स्वाहा

Namaskar to the Mother, the Supporter of all.

660. ॐ सुप्रतिष्ठायै नमः
ॐ सुप्रतिष्ठायै स्वाहा

Namaskar to the Well established Mother.

661. ॐ सदसद्रूपधारिण्यै नमः
ॐ सद्-असद्-रूप-धारिण्यै स्वाहा

Namaskar to the Mother, who is the form of being and non-being.

662. ॐ अष्टमूर्त्यै नमः
ॐ अष्ट-मूर्त्यै स्वाहा

Namaskar to the Mother having Eight forms.

663. ॐ अजाजेत्र्यै नमः
ॐ अजा-जेत्र्यै स्वाहा

Namaskar to the Mother, in the conqueror of the unborn.

664. ॐ लोकयात्राविधायिन्यै नमः
ॐ लोक-यात्रा-विधायिन्यै स्वाहा

Namaskar to the Mother, who Directs the course of the worlds.

665. ॐ एकाकिन्यै नमः
ॐ एकाकिन्यै स्वाहा

Namaskar to the Solitary one Mother.

666. ॐ भूमरूपायै नमः
ॐ भूम-रूपायै स्वाहा

Namaskar to the Mother who is the self of Bhuma – an aggregate of all that exists.

667. ॐ निर्द्वैतायै नमः
ॐ निर्द्वैतायै स्वाहा

Namaskar to the Mother, who is without duality.

668. ॐ द्वैतवर्जितायै नमः
ॐ द्वैत-वर्जितायै स्वाहा

Namaskar to the Mother, who transcends duality.

669. ॐ अन्नदायै नमः
ॐ अन्नदायै स्वाहा

Namaskar to the Mother, who is the Giver of food.

670. ॐ वसुदायै नमः
ॐ वसुदायै स्वाहा

Namaskar to the Mother, who is the Giver of wealth.

671. ॐ वृद्धायै नमः
ॐ वृद्धायै स्वाहा

Namaskar to the oldest Mother.

672. ॐ ब्रह्मात्मैक्य स्वरूपिण्यै नमः
ॐ ब्रह्म-आत्म-एक्य-स्वरूपिण्यै स्वाहा

Namaskar to the Mother, who is the union of Brahman and Atman.

673. ॐ बृहत्यै नमः
ॐ बृहत्यै स्वाहा

Namaskar to the Great Mother.

674. ॐ ब्राह्मण्यै नमः
ॐ ब्राह्मण्यै स्वाहा

Namaskar to the Mother Brahmani – medicinal plant.

675. ॐ ब्राह्मयै नमः
ॐ ब्राह्मयै स्वाहा

Namaskar to the Mother Brahmi – the consort of Brahma.

676. ॐ ब्रह्मानन्दायै नमः
ॐ ब्रह्मानन्दायै स्वाहा

Namaskar to the Mother, who is the Bliss of Brahman.

677. ॐ बलिप्रियायै नमः
ॐ बलि-प्रियायै स्वाहा

Namaskar to the Mother, who likes sacrifice.

678. ॐ भाषारूपायै नमः
ॐ भाषा-रूपायै स्वाहा

Namaskar to the Mother Language – the Mother tongue.

679. ॐ बृहत्सेनायै नमः
ॐ बृहत्-सेनायै स्वाहा

Namaskar to the Mother, who is with Mighty arms.

680. ॐ भावभावविवर्जितायै नमः
ॐ भाव-अभाव-विवर्जितायै स्वाहा

Namaskar to the Mother, who is devoid of the positive and negative entities.

681. ॐ सुखाराध्यायै नमः
ॐ सुख-आराध्यायै स्वाहा

Namaskar to the Mother, who can be Easily worshipped.

682. ॐ शुभकर्यै नमः
ॐ शुभकर्यै स्वाहा

Namaskar to the Mother, who always does Good.

683. ॐ शोभनायै सुलभायै गत्यै नमः
ॐ शोभनायै-सुलभायै-गत्यै स्वाहा

Namaskar to the Mother, who can be easily attained by the Right approach.

684. ॐ राजराजेश्वर्यै नमः
ॐ राज-राजेश्वर्यै स्वाहा

Namaskar to the Mother Rajarajeshwari – the Supreme Sovereign King.

685. ॐ राज्यदायिन्यै नमः
ॐ राज्य-दायिन्यै स्वाहा

Namaskar to the Mother the Bestower of kingdom.

686. ॐ राज्यवल्लभायै नमः
ॐ राज्य-वल्लभायै स्वाहा

Namaskar to the Mother, who is Delighted in dominion of states.

687. ॐ राजत्कृपायै नमः
ॐ राजत्-कृपायै स्वाहा

Namaskar to the Mother, whose Mercy is Superb.

688. ॐ राजपीठनिवेशितनिजाश्रितायै नमः
ॐ राजपीठ-निवेशित-निज-आश्रितायै स्वाहा

Namaskar to the Mother, whose dependants are established in thrones.

689. ॐ राज्यलक्ष्म्यै नमः
ॐ राज्य-लक्ष्म्यै स्वाहा

Namaskar to the Mother Rajyalakshami – the State wealth.

690. ॐ कोशनाथाय नमः
ॐ कोश-नाथाय स्वाहा

Namaskar to the Mother, who is the Mistress of Royal treasury.

691. ॐ चतुरङ्ग बलेश्वर्यै नमः
ॐ चतुरङ्ग-बलेश्वर्यै स्वाहा

Namaskar to the Mother, who is the Supreme Commander of Chaturanga forces-cavalry, elephants, chariots and infantry.

692. ॐ साम्राज्यदायिन्यै नमः
ॐ साम्राज्य-दायिन्यै स्वाहा

Namaskar to the Mother, the Bestower of empire.

693. ॐ सत्यसन्ध्यायै नमः
ॐ सत्य-सन्ध्यायै स्वाहा

Namaskar to the Mother, who is Devoted to truth.

694. ॐ सागरमेखलायै नमः
ॐ सागर-मेखलायै स्वाहा

Namaskar to the Mother, who is Girdled by Ocean.

695. ॐ दीक्षितायै नमः
ॐ दीक्षितायै स्वाहा

Namaskar to the Initiated Mother.

696. ॐ दैत्यशमन्यै नमः
ॐ दैत्य-शमन्यै स्वाहा

Namaskar to the Mother the Controller of Daityas – Bhandasura etc.

697. ॐ सर्वलोकवशंकर्यै नमः
ॐ सर्व-लोक-वशंकर्यै स्वाहा

Namaskar to the Mother, who Subjugates all the worlds.

698. ॐ सर्वार्थदात्र्यै नमः
ॐ सर्वार्थ-दात्र्यै स्वाहा

Namaskar to the Mother, who Bestows all objects.

699. ॐ सावित्र्यै नमः
ॐ सावित्र्यै स्वाहा

Namaskar to the Mother Savitri – the Solar energy.

700. ॐ सच्चिदानन्दरूपिण्यै नमः
ॐ सत्-चित्-आनन्द-रूपिण्यै स्वाहा

Namaskar to the Mother, who is Existence, consciousness and bliss.

701. ॐ देशकालापरिच्छिन्नायै नमः
ॐ देश-काल-अपरिच्छिन्नायै स्वाहा

Namaskar to the Mother, who is Unlimited by space and time.

702. ॐ सर्वगायै नमः
ॐ सर्वगायै स्वाहा

Namaskar to the Omnipresent Mother.

703. ॐ सर्वमोहिन्यै नमः
ॐ सर्व-मोहिन्यै स्वाहा

Namaskar to the All-bewildering Mother.

704. ॐ सरस्वत्यै नमः
ॐ सरस्वत्यै स्वाहा

Namaskar to the Mother Sarasvati.

705. ॐ शास्त्रमय्यै नमः
ॐ शास्त्र-मय्यै स्वाहा

Namaskar to the Mother Scripture.

706. ॐ गुहाम्बायै नमः
ॐ गुहा-अम्बायै स्वाहा

Namaskar to the Mother Cavity in holes of the Earth.

707. ॐ गुह्यरूपिण्यै नमः
ॐ गुह्य-रूपिण्यै स्वाहा

Namaskar to the Mother, who is having the Secret form.

708. ॐ सर्वोपाधिविनिर्मुक्तायै नमः
ॐ सर्व-उपाधि-विनिर्मुक्तायै स्वाहा

Namaskar to the Mother, who is Free from all limitations.

709. ॐ सदाशिवपतिव्रतायै नमः
ॐ सदा-शिव-पतिव्रतायै स्वाहा

Namaskar to the Mother, who has vowed that Siva alone is Her Spouse.

710. ॐ सम्प्रदायेश्वर्यै नमः
ॐ सम्प्रदायेश्वर्यै स्वाहा

Namaskar to the Mother, who is the Primal tradition.

711. ॐ साधुने नमः
ॐ साधुने स्वाहा

Namaskar to the Mother with excellent deed.

712. ॐ यै नमः
ॐ यै स्वाहा

Namaskar to the Mother 'I' – the fourth vowel or transcendental state.

713. ॐ गुरुमण्डलरूपिण्यै नमः
ॐ गुरुमण्डल-रूपिण्यै स्वाहा

Namaskar to the Mother, who is in formative aspect of the Spiritual teachers.

714. ॐ कुलोत्तीर्णाय नमः
ॐ कुल-उत्तीर्णाय स्वाहा

Namaskar to the Mother, who has transcended the group of senses.

715. ॐ भगाराध्यायै नमः
ॐ भग-आराध्यायै स्वाहा

Namaskar to the Mother, who is worshipped in the sun.

716. ॐ मायायै नमः
ॐ मायायै स्वाहा

Namaskar to the Mother Maya – the Supreme power of Creativity.

717. ॐ मधुमत्यै नमः
ॐ मधुमत्यै स्वाहा

Namaskar to the Mother Madhumati–river.

718. ॐ मह्यै नमः
ॐ मह्यै स्वाहा

Namaskar to the Mother Earth.

719. ॐ गणाम्बायै नमः
ॐ गण-अम्बायै स्वाहा

Namaskar to the Mother of followers of Siva and Ganesha.

720. ॐ गुह्यकाराध्यायै नमः
ॐ गुह्यकाराध्यायै स्वाहा

Namaskar to the Mother, who is worshipped in the Secret place.

721. ॐ कोमलाङ्गायै नमः
ॐ कोमल-अङ्गायै स्वाहा

Namaskar to the Tender-limbed Mother.

722. ॐ गुरुप्रियायै नमः
ॐ गुरु-प्रियायै स्वाहा

Namaskar to the Mother to whom the Guru is very dear.

723. ॐ स्वतंत्रायै नमः
ॐ स्वतंत्रायै स्वाहा

Namaskar to the Independent Mother.

724. ॐ सर्वतंत्रेश्यै नमः
ॐ सर्व-तंत्रेश्यै स्वाहा

Namaskar to the Mother, who is the Ruler of all the Tantras – being sixty four in number.

725. ॐ दक्षिणामूर्तिरूपिण्यै नमः
ॐ दक्षिणामूर्ति-रूपिण्यै स्वाहा

Namaskar to the Mother in the form of Dakshinamurti.

726. ॐ सनकादिसमाराध्यायै नमः
ॐ सनकादि-समाराध्यायै स्वाहा

Namaskar to the Mother to whom Sanak and other (Gurus) worship.

727. ॐ शिवज्ञानप्रदायिन्यै नमः
ॐ शिव-ज्ञान-प्रदायिन्यै स्वाहा

Namaskar to the Mother, who imparts the Supreme knowledge of Shiva, aspect of Reality.

728. ॐ चित्कलायै नमः
ॐ चित्-कलायै स्वाहा

Namaskar to the Mother Chitakala – Consciousness aspect of Reality.

729. ॐ आनन्दकालिकायै नमः
ॐ आनन्द-कलिकायै स्वाहा

Namaskar to the Mother, who is the Bud of bliss.

730. ॐ प्रेमरूपायै नमः
ॐ प्रेम-रूपायै स्वाहा

Namaskar to the Affectionate Mother.

731. ॐ प्रियङ्कर्यै नमः
ॐ प्रियङ्कर्यै स्वाहा

Namaskar to the Mother, who is the cause of affection.

732. ॐ नामपरायणप्रीतायै नमः
ॐ नामपरायण-प्रीतायै स्वाहा

Namaskar to the Mother, who gets delighted in the repetition of Her names.

733. ॐ नन्दिविद्यायै नमः
ॐ नन्दि-विद्यायै स्वाहा

Namaskar to the Mother, who is the Vidya aspect worshipped by Nandi.

734. ॐ नटेश्वर्यै नमः
ॐ नटेश्वर्यै स्वाहा

Namaskar to the Mother, who is the consort of the Dancer Nataraja.

735. ॐ मिथ्याजगदधिष्ठानायै नमः
ॐ मिथ्या-जगत्-अधिष्ठानायै स्वाहा

Namaskar to the Mother, who is the Basis of the illusory Universe.

736. ॐ मुक्तिदायै नमः
ॐ मुक्ति-दायै स्वाहा

Namaskar to the Mother, who grants salvation.

737. ॐ मुक्तिरूपिण्यै नमः
ॐ मुक्ति-रूपिण्यै स्वाहा

Namaskar to the Mother in the form of salvation.

738. ॐ लास्यप्रियायै नमः
ॐ लास्य-प्रियायै स्वाहा

Namaskar to the Mother, who is fond of the rhythemic dance.

739. ॐ लयकर्यै नमः
ॐ लयकर्यै स्वाहा

Namaskar to the Mother, who causes absorption.

740. ॐ लज्जायै नमः
ॐ लज्जायै स्वाहा

Namaskar to the Mother Modesty.

741. ॐ रम्भादिवन्दितायै नमः
ॐ रम्भा-आदि-वन्दितायै स्वाहा

Namaskar to the Mother, who is adored by Rambha and other heavenly damsels.

742. ॐ भवदावसुधावृष्टयै नमः
ॐ भव-दाव-सुधा-वृष्टयै स्वाहा

Namaskar to the Mother Rain in the form of nectar falling in the forest fire of the worldly existence.

743. ॐ पापारण्यदावानलायै नमः
ॐ पापारण्य-दावानलायै स्वाहा

Namaskar to the Mother Forest Fire, who consumes the wood land of sins.

744. ॐ दौर्भाग्यतूलवातुलायै नमः
ॐ दौर्भाग्य-तूल-वातुलायै स्वाहा

Namaskar to the Mother, who drives away want and misfortune like whirlwind.

745. ॐ जराध्वान्तरविप्रभायै नमः
ॐ जरा-ध्वान्त-रवि-प्रभायै स्वाहा

Namaskar to the Mother Sun beam, who dispells darkness and dismay.

746. ॐ भाग्याबिधचन्द्रिकायै नमः
ॐ भाग्याबिध-चन्द्रिकायै स्वाहा

Namaskar to the Mother Moon beam, who is the Ocean of good fortune.

747. ॐ भक्तचित्तकेकिघनाघनायै नमः
ॐ भक्त-चित्त-केकि-घनाघनायै स्वाहा

Namaskar to the Mother cloud, who continuously nourishes the consciousness of her devotees.

748. ॐ रोगपर्वतदम्भोलये नमः
ॐ रोग-पर्वत-दम्भोलये स्वाहा

Namaskar to the Mother Thunderbolt, which destroys the mountain of diseases.

749. ॐ मृत्युदारुकुठारिकायै नमः
ॐ मृत्यु-दारु-कुठारिकायै स्वाहा

Namaskar to the Mother Axe, that cuts down the tree of death.

750. ॐ महेश्वर्यै नमः
ॐ महेश्वर्यै स्वाहा

Namaskar to the Mother Maheshvari–the Sovereign Supreme.

751. ॐ महाकाल्यै नमः
ॐ महा-काल्यै स्वाहा

Namaskar to the Mother Maha-Kali.

752. ॐ महाग्रासायै नमः
ॐ महा-ग्रासायै स्वाहा

Namaskar to the Mother, who is Great devourer.

753. ॐ महाशनायै नमः
ॐ महाशनायै स्वाहा

Namaskar to the Mother, who consumes everything.

754. ॐ अपर्णायै नमः
ॐ अपर्णायै स्वाहा

Namaskar to the Mother Aparna - who does not take even a leaf.

755. ॐ चण्डिकायै नमः
ॐ चण्डिकायै स्वाहा

Namaskar to the Mother Chandika - ferocious one.

756. ॐ चण्डमुण्डासुरनिषूदन्यै नमः
ॐ चण्ड-मुण्ड-असुर-निषूदन्यै स्वाहा

Namaskar to the Mother, who is the Destroyer of Chanda and Munda Asuras.

757. ॐ क्षराक्षरात्मिकायै नमः
ॐ क्षर-अक्षर-आत्मिकायै स्वाहा

Namaskar to the Perishable and Imperishable Mother.

758. ॐ सर्वलोकेश्यै नमः
ॐ सर्व-लोकेश्यै स्वाहा

Namaskar to the Mother, who is the Ruler of all worlds.

759. ॐ विश्वधारिण्यै नमः
ॐ विश्व-धारिण्यै स्वाहा

Namaskar to the Mother, who is the Supporter of the universe.

760. ॐ त्रिवर्गदात्र्यै नमः
ॐ त्रिवर्ग-दात्र्यै स्वाहा

Namaskar to the Mother, who is the Giver of three objects of desire.

761. ॐ सुभगायै नमः
ॐ सुभगायै स्वाहा

Namaskar to the Mother of Good fortune.

762. ॐ त्र्यम्बकायै नमः
ॐ त्र्यम्बकायै स्वाहा

Namaskar to the Mother Tryambaka – the three-eyed.

763. ॐ त्रिगुणात्मिकायै नमः
ॐ त्रिगुण-आत्मिकायै स्वाहा

Namaskar to the Mother, who has three attributes.

764. ॐ स्वर्गापवर्गदायै नमः
ॐ स्वर्ग-अपवर्ग-दायै स्वाहा

Namaskar to the Mother, who bestows heaven and salvation.

765. ॐ शुद्धायै नमः
ॐ शुद्धायै स्वाहा

Namaskar to the Pure Mother.

766. ॐ जपापुष्पनिभाकृतयै नमः
ॐ जपा-पुष्प-निभा-आकृतये स्वाहा

Namaskar to the Mother, whose body is that of the hibiscus flower – China rose.

767. ॐ ओजोवत्यै नमः
ॐ ओजोवत्यै स्वाहा

Namaskar to the Mother Ojovati–the Vitality.

768. ॐ द्युतिधरायै नमः
ॐ द्युति-धरायै स्वाहा

Namaskar to the Mother, who is the Bearer of brilliance.

769. ॐ यज्ञरूपायै नमः
ॐ यज्ञ-रूपायै स्वाहा

Namaskar to the Mother Sacrifice.

770. ॐ प्रियव्रतायै नमः
ॐ प्रिय-व्रतायै स्वाहा

Namaskar to the Mother, who is fond of vows.

771. ॐ दुराराध्यायै नमः
ॐ दुराराध्यायै स्वाहा

Namaskar to the Mother, who can be worshipped only with great difficulty.

772. ॐ दुराधर्षायै नमः
ॐ दुराधर्षायै स्वाहा

Namaskar to the Mother Resistance.

773. ॐ पाटलीकुसुमप्रियायै नमः
ॐ पाटली-कुसुम-प्रियायै स्वाहा

Namaskar to the Mother, who is fond of Patali flowers.

774. ॐ महत्यै नमः
ॐ महत्यै स्वाहा

Namaskar to the Mother Excellence.

775. ॐ मेरुनिलयायै नमः
ॐ मेरु-निलयायै स्वाहा

Namaskar to the Mother, who resides on the mount Meru

776. ॐ मन्दारकुसुमप्रियायै नमः
ॐ मन्दार-कुसुम-प्रियायै स्वाहा

Namaskar to the Mother, to whom the 'Mandar' flowers are very dear.

777. ॐ वीराराध्यायै नमः
ॐ वीर-आराध्यायै स्वाहा

Namaskar to the Mother, who is worshipped by Warriors.

778. ॐ विराड्रूपायै नमः
ॐ विराट-रूपायै स्वाहा

Namaskar to the Mother Viratrupa–form of Universe.

779. ॐ विरजसे नमः

ॐ विरजसे स्वाहा

Namaskar to the Passionless Mother.

780. ॐ विश्वतोमुख्यै नमः

ॐ विश्वतो-मुख्यै स्वाहा

Namaskar to the Mother, who is facing everywhere and direction.

781. ॐ प्रत्यग्रूपायै नमः

ॐ प्रत्यक्-रूपायै स्वाहा

Namaskar to the Mother Interior.

782. ॐ पराकाशायै नमः

ॐ पराकाशायै स्वाहा

Namaskar to the Supreme Mother Ether.

783. ॐ प्राणदायै नमः

ॐ प्राण-दायै स्वाहा

Namaskar to the Mother, the giver of vital breath.

784. ॐ प्राणरूपिण्यै नमः

ॐ प्राण-रूपिण्यै स्वाहा

Namaskar to the Mother, in the form of Vital breath.

785. ॐ मार्ताण्डभैरवाराध्यायै नमः

ॐ मार्ताण्ड-भैरव-आराध्यायै स्वाहा

Namaskar to the Mother, who is adored by the Martandabhairva – the Solar system.

786. ॐ मन्त्रिणीन्यस्तराज्यधुरे नमः

ॐ मन्त्रिणी-न्यस्त-राज्य-धुरे स्वाहा

Namaskar to the Mother, who has entrusted her kingdom to Mantrini–the Mantra force or Shyamlambha.

787. ॐ त्रिपुरेश्यै नमः

ॐ त्रि-पुरेश्यै स्वाहा

Namaskar to the Mother Tripureshi – the Sixteen-petalled sarvaasha paripurak Chakra of Sri Yantra.

788. ॐ जयत्सेनायै नमः
ॐ जयत्-सेनायै स्वाहा

Namaskar to the Mother, who has got victorious army.

789. ॐ निस्त्रैगुण्यायै नमः
ॐ निः त्रैगुण्यायै स्वाहा

Namaskar to the Mother, who is devoid of the three qualities.

790. ॐ परापरायै नमः
ॐ पर-अपरायै स्वाहा

Namaskar to the Highest and the Lowest Mother.

791. ॐ सत्यज्ञानानन्दरूपायै नमः
ॐ सत्य-ज्ञान-आनन्द-रूपायै स्वाहा

Namaskar to the True, Wise and Blissful Mother.

792. ॐ सामरस्यपरायणायै नमः
ॐ साम-रस्य परायणायै स्वाहा

Namaskar to the Mother of Harmony, who is deeply interested in the unchanging unity of Jiva and Shiva.

793. ॐ कपर्दिन्यै नमः
ॐ कपर्दिन्यै स्वाहा

Namaskar to Her, who is the Consort of Kapardin (Shiva) the sanctifier of the water flow of Ganga.

794. ॐ कलामालायै नमः
ॐ कला-मालायै स्वाहा

Namaskar to the Mother-craft, having garlanded the sixty four arts.

795. ॐ कामदुधे नमः
ॐ काम-दुधे स्वाहा

Namaskar to the Mother Kamadhenu – the cow of plenty.

796. ॐ कामरूपिण्यै नमः
ॐ काम-रूपिण्यै स्वाहा

Namaskar to the Mother Desire.

797. ॐ कलानिधये नमः

ॐ कला-निधये स्वाहा

Namaskar to the Mother Treasure of Sciences.

798. ॐ काव्यकलायै नमः

ॐ काव्य-कलायै स्वाहा।

Namaskar to the Mother Poetics.

799. ॐ रसज्ञायै नमः

ॐ रस-ज्ञायै स्वाहा

Namaskar to the Mother Drama.

800. ॐ रसशेवधये नमः

ॐ रस-शेवधये स्वाहा

Namaskar to the Mother, who is the treasure house of Rasa.

801. ॐ पुष्टायै नमः

ॐ पुष्टायै स्वाहा

Namaskar to the Mother Nourishment.

802. ॐ पुरातनायै नमः

ॐ पुरातनायै स्वाहा

Namaskar to the Ancient Mother.

803. ॐ पूज्यायै नमः

ॐ पूज्यायै स्वाहा

Namaskar to the Mother, who is revered by all.

804. ॐ पुष्करायै नमः

ॐ पुष्करायै स्वाहा

Namaskar to the Lotus Mother.

805. ॐ पुष्करेक्षणायै नमः

ॐ पुष्कर-ईक्षणायै स्वाहा

Namaskar to the Lotus-eyed Mother.

806. ॐ परस्मै ज्योतिषे नमः

ॐ परस्मै ज्योतिषे स्वाहा

Namaskar to the Mother of Supreme Light.

807. ॐ परस्मै धाम्ने नमः
ॐ परस्मै धाम्ने स्वाहा

Namaskar to the Mother of Supreme abode.

808. ॐ परमाणवे नमः
ॐ परम्-आणवे स्वाहा

Namaskar to the Mother found in Supreme atom.

809. ॐ परात्परायै नमः
ॐ परात्परायै स्वाहा

Namaskar to the Supermost Supreme Mother.

810. ॐ पाशहस्तायै नमः
ॐ पाशहस्तायै स्वाहा

Namaskar to the Mother bearing a noose in her hand.

811. ॐ पाशहन्त्र्यै नमः
ॐ पाशहन्त्र्यै स्वाहा

Namaskar to the Mother, who is herself the Destroyer of noose.

812. ॐ परमंत्रविभेदिन्यै नमः
ॐ पर-मंत्र-विभेदिन्यै स्वाहा

Namaskar to the Mother, who destroys the hostile spells of magic.

813. ॐ मूर्तायै नमः
ॐ मूर्तायै स्वाहा

Namaskar to the Mother Form – manifest universe.

814. ॐ अमूर्तायै नमः
ॐ अमूर्तायै स्वाहा

Namaskar to the Formless Mother.

815. ॐ अनित्यतृप्तायै नमः
ॐ अनित्य-तृप्तायै स्वाहा

Namaskar to the Mother, who is satisfied with the perishable.

816. ॐ मुनिमानसहंसिकायै नमः
ॐ मुनि-मानस-हंसिकायै स्वाहा

Namaskar to the Mother Swan of the Manasa lake of the mind of Muni.

817. ॐ सत्यव्रतायै नमः
ॐ सत्यव्रतायै स्वाहा

Namaskar to the Mother of fixed vows.

818. ॐ सत्यरूपायै नमः
ॐ सत्य-रूपायै स्वाहा

Namaskar to the Mother Reality.

819. ॐ सर्वान्तर्यामिन्यै नमः
ॐ सर्वान्तयर्-यामिन्यै स्वाहा

Namaskar to the Mother pervading in all hearts.

820. ॐ सत्यै नमः
ॐ सत्यै स्वाहा

Namaskar to the Mother Sati–daughter of Daksha.

821. ॐ ब्रह्माण्यै नमः
ॐ ब्रह्माण्यै स्वाहा

Namaskar to the Mother Brahmani – Creator of Brahma.

822. ॐ ब्रह्मणे नमः
ॐ ब्रह्मणे स्वाहा

Namaskar to the Mother Brahman – Supreme Word.

823. ॐ जनन्यै नमः
ॐ जनन्यै स्वाहा

Namaskar to the Mother – the Creator of the whole Universe.

824. ॐ बहुरूपायै नमः
ॐ बहु-रूपायै स्वाहा

Namaskar to the Mother in manifold forms.

825. ॐ बुधार्चितायै नमः
ॐ बुध-अर्चितायै स्वाहा

Namaskar to the Mother, who is adored by the wise.

826. ॐ प्रसवित्र्यै नमः
ॐ प्रसवित्र्यै स्वाहा

Namaskar to the Creative Mother.

827. ॐ प्रचण्डायै नमः
ॐ प्रचण्डायै स्वाहा

Namaskar to the Wrathful Mother.

828. ॐ आज्ञायै नमः
ॐ आज्ञायै स्वाहा

Namaskar to the Mother Command–Supreme dictates.

829. ॐ प्रतिष्ठायै नमः
ॐ प्रतिष्ठायै स्वाहा

Namaskar to the Mother Foundation.

830. ॐ प्रकटाकृतये नमः
ॐ प्रकट-आकृतये स्वाहा

Namaskar to the Mother Obvious in form.

831. ॐ प्राणेश्वर्यै नमः
ॐ प्राण-ईश्वर्यै स्वाहा

Namaskar to the Mother as Lord of senses.

832. ॐ प्राणदात्र्यै नमः
ॐ प्राण-दात्र्यै स्वाहा

Namaskar to the Mother as Nourisher of senses.

833. ॐ पञ्चाशत्पीठरूपिण्यै नमः
ॐ पञ्चाशत्-पीठ-रूपिण्यै स्वाहा

Namaskar to the Mother in the form of Fifty seats.

834. ॐ विश्रृङ्खलायै नमः
ॐ विश्रृङ्खलायै स्वाहा

Namaskar to the Unbonded Mother.

835. ॐ विविक्तस्थायै नमः
ॐ विविक्तस्थायै स्वाहा

Namaskar to the Mother who abides in Lonely places.

836. ॐ वीरमात्रे नमः
ॐ वीर-मात्रे स्वाहा
Namaskar to the Viramata–the Mother of Warriors.

837. ॐ वियत्प्रसुवे नमः
ॐ वियत्-प्रसुवे स्वाहा
Namaskar to the Mother of Space.

838. ॐ मुकुन्दायै नमः
ॐ मुकुन्दायै स्वाहा
Namaskar to the Mother Mukunda - Vaishnavi.

839. ॐ मुक्तिनिलयायै नमः
ॐ मुक्ति-निलयायै स्वाहा
Namaskar to the Mother, whose abode is Salvation.

840. ॐ मूलविग्रहरूपिण्यै नमः
ॐ मूल-विग्रह-रूपिण्यै स्वाहा
Namaskar to the Mother, whose body is the Root.

841. ॐ भावज्ञायै नमः
ॐ भाव-ज्ञायै स्वाहा
Namaskar to the Mother Knower of Thought.

842. ॐ भवरोगहन्त्यै नमः
ॐ भव-रोगहन्त्यै स्वाहा
Namaskar to the Mother, who destroys the pains of earthly existence.

843. ॐ भवचक्रप्रवर्तिन्यै नमः
ॐ भव-चक्र-प्रवर्तिन्यै स्वाहा
Namaskar to the Mother, who turns the wheel of earthly existence.

844. ॐ छन्दःसारायै नमः
ॐ छन्दः-सारायै स्वाहा
Namaskar to the Mother of the Science of metres.

845. ॐ शास्त्रसारायै नमः
ॐ शास्त्र-सारायै स्वाहा
Namaskar to the Mother Essence of the scriptures.

846. ॐ मन्त्रसारायै नमः
ॐ मन्त्र-सारायै स्वाहा

Namaskar to the Mother Essence of the Mantras.

847. ॐ तलोदर्यै नमः
ॐ तल-उदर्यै स्वाहा

Namaskar to the Slender waisted Mother.

848. ॐ उदारकीर्त्यै नमः
ॐ उदार-कीर्त्यै स्वाहा

Namaskar to the Mother of the Exalted fame.

849. ॐ उद्दामवैभवायै नमः
ॐ उद्दाम-वैभवायै स्वाहा

Namaskar to the Mother, whose Glory is exalted.

850. ॐ वर्णरूपिण्यै नमः
ॐ वर्ण-रूपिण्यै स्वाहा

Namaskar to the Mother Alphabet.

851. ॐ जन्ममुत्युजरातप्तजनविश्रान्तिदायिन्यै नमः
ॐ जन्म-मुत्यु-जरा-तप्त-जन-विश्रान्ति-दायिन्यै स्वाहा

Namaskar to the Mother, who grants birth, death, oldage and happiness.

852. ॐ सर्वोपनिषदुघुष्टायै नमः
ॐ सर्वोपनिषत्-उदुघुष्टायै स्वाहा

Namaskar to the Mother, who is Proclaimed by all the Upanishads.

853. ॐ शान्त्यीतकलात्मिकायै नमः
ॐ शान्ति-अतीत-कला-आत्मिकायै स्वाहा

Namaskar to the Shantitya-Kala Mother – the Super-cosmic power transcending place.

854. ॐ गम्भीरायै नमः
ॐ गम्भीरायै स्वाहा

Namaskar to the Fathomless Mother.

855. ॐ गगनान्तः स्थायै नमः
ॐ गगनान्तः स्थायै स्वाहा

Namaskar to the Mother, who resides in the ether.

856. ॐ गर्वितायै नमः
ॐ गर्वितायै स्वाहा

Namaskar to the Proud Mother.

857. ॐ गानलोलुपायै नमः
ॐ गान-लोलुपायै स्वाहा

Namaskar to the Mother, who gets delighted in the songs.

858. ॐ कल्पनारहितायै नमः
ॐ कल्पना-रहितायै स्वाहा

Namaskar to the Mother, who is devoid of any imagination.

859. ॐ काष्ठायै नमः
ॐ काष्ठायै स्वाहा

Namaskar to the Mother Kashtha–the Spouse of Supreme Shiva-Ultimate Goal.

860. ॐ अकान्तायै नमः
ॐ अकान्तायै स्वाहा

Namaskar to the Mother Akanta – ignorance and delusion.

861. ॐ कान्तार्धविग्रहायै नमः
ॐ कान्तार्ध-विग्रहायै स्वाहा

Namaskar to the Mother, who is the half part of Supreme Shiva.

862. ॐ कार्यकारणनिर्मुक्तायै नमः
ॐ कार्य-कारण-निर्मुक्तायै स्वाहा

Namaskar to the Mother, who is Free from cause and effect.

863. ॐ कामकेलितरङ्गितायै नमः
ॐ काम-केलि-तरङ्गितायै स्वाहा

Namaskar to the Mother, who is outflowing with desire and pleasure.

864. ॐ कनत्कनकताटङ्कायै नमः

ॐ कनत्-कनक-ताटङ्कायै स्वाहा

Namaskar to the Mother, who is wearing shining golden ear-rings.

865. ॐ लीलाविग्रहधारिण्यै नमः

ॐ लीला-विग्रह-धारिण्यै स्वाहा

Namaskar to the Mother, who assumes various incarnations, merely for Sport.

866. ॐ अजायै नमः

ॐ अजायै स्वाहा

Namaskar to the Unborn Mother.

867. ॐ क्षयविनिर्मुक्तायै नमः

ॐ क्षय-विनिर्मुक्तायै स्वाहा

Namaskar to the Mother who is free from decay.

868. ॐ मुग्धायै नमः

ॐ मुग्धायै स्वाहा

Namaskar to the Attractive Mother.

869. ॐ क्षिप्रप्रसादिन्यै नमः

ॐ क्षिप्र-प्रसादिन्यै स्वाहा

Namaskar to the Mother, who gets easily pleased.

870. ॐ अन्तर्मुखसमाराध्यायै नमः

ॐ अन्तः-मुख-समाराध्यायै स्वाहा

Namaskar to the Mother, who is worshipped internally.

871. ॐ बहिर्मुखसुदुर्लभायै नमः

ॐ बहिः मुख-सुदुर्लभायै स्वाहा

Namaskar to the Mother, whose attainment in extremely heard by those, who are devoted to external objects.

872. ॐ त्रय्यै नमः

ॐ त्रय्यै स्वाहा

Namaskar to the Mother Trayyi–Veda Mata.

873. ॐ त्रिवर्गनिलयायै नमः
ॐ त्रिवर्ग-निलयायै स्वाहा

Namaskar to the Mother, who is the abode of Tri-Varga i.e. Dharma, Artha, Kama.

874. ॐ त्रिस्थायै नमः
ॐ त्रिस्थायै स्वाहा

Namaskar to the Mother, who resides in 'Triple form' – AUM.

875. ॐ त्रिपुरमालिन्यै नमः
ॐ त्रिपुर-मालिन्यै स्वाहा

Namaskar to the Mother Tripura malini-Antardashara region of Sri Chakra.

876. ॐ निरामयायै नमः
ॐ निरामायायै स्वाहा

Namaskar to the Mother, who is free from any disease.

877. ॐ निरालम्बायै नमः
ॐ निरालम्बायै स्वाहा

Namaskar to the Mother, who needs no Support.

878. ॐ स्वात्मारामायै नमः
ॐ स्वात्मारामायै स्वाहा

Namaskar to the Mother, who rejoices in Herself.

879. ॐ सुधास्रुत्यै नमः
ॐ सुधास्रुत्यै स्वाहा

Namaskar to the Mother, who is Stream of nectar.

880. ॐ संसारपङ्कनिर्मग्नसमुद्धरणपण्डितायै नमः
ॐ संसार-पङ्क-निर्मग्न-समुद्धरण-पण्डितायै स्वाहा

Namaskar to the Proficient Mother, who pulls out those, who are sunk in the worldly mud.

881. ॐ यज्ञप्रियायै नमः
ॐ यज्ञ-प्रियायै स्वाहा

Namaskar to the Mother, who is fond of sacrifice.

882. ॐ यज्ञकर्त्र्यै नमः
ॐ यज्ञ-कर्त्र्यै स्वाहा

Namaskar to the Mother, who is the doer of Sacrifice.

883. ॐ यजमानस्वरूपिण्यै नमः
ॐ यजमान-स्वरूपिण्यै स्वाहा

Namaskar to the Mother, who is the very person of Sacrificer.

884. ॐ धर्माधारायै नमः
ॐ धर्म-आधारायै स्वाहा

Namaskar to the Mother, who supports Dharma.

885. ॐ धनाध्यक्षायै नमः
ॐ धनाध्यक्षायै स्वाहा

Namaskar to the Presiding Mother of Wealth.

886. ॐ धनधान्यविवर्धिन्यै नमः
ॐ धन-धान्य-विवर्धिन्यै स्वाहा

Namaskar to the Mother, who increases wealth and granary.

887. ॐ विप्रप्रियायै नमः
ॐ विप्र-प्रियायै स्वाहा

Namaskar to the lovely Mother of 'twice-born' the possessors of Vedic knowledge.

888. ॐ विप्ररूपायै नमः
ॐ विप्र-रूपायै स्वाहा

Namaskar to the Mother, who is the very form of Vipras–the twice born.

889. ॐ विश्वभ्रमणकारिण्यै नमः
ॐ विश्व-भ्रमण-कारिण्यै स्वाहा

Namaskar to the Mother, who causes the revolution of the Universe.

890. ॐ विश्वग्रासायै नमः
ॐ विश्व-ग्रासायै स्वाहा

Namaskar to the Mother, who Consumes the Universe.

891. ॐ विद्रुमाभायै नमः
ॐ विद्रुमाभायै स्वाहा

Namaskar to the Mother, who is of the Colour of Coral.

892. ॐ वैष्णव्यै नमः
ॐ वैष्णव्यै स्वाहा

Namaskar to the Mother Vaishnavi.

893. ॐ विष्णुरूपिण्यै नमः
ॐ विष्णु-रूपिण्यै स्वाहा

Namaskar to the Mother, who is in the form of Vishnu.

894. ॐ अयोनयै नमः
ॐ अयोनयै स्वाहा

Namaskar to the Mother, who has no Origin.

895. ॐ योनिनिलयायै नमः
ॐ योनि-निलयायै स्वाहा

Namaskar to the Mother, who resides in Yoni – Cause of the Universe.

896. ॐ कूटस्थायै नमः
ॐ कूटस्थायै स्वाहा

Namaskar to the Mother, who governs 'Kutas' – the multitude of Universes.

897. ॐ कुलरूपिण्यै नमः
ॐ कुल-रूपिण्यै स्वाहा

Namaskar to the Mother Kularupini – the form of 'Kula' system of Tantrik worship.

898. ॐ वीरगोष्ठीप्रियायै नमः
ॐ वीर-गोष्ठी-प्रियायै स्वाहा

Namaskar to the Mother, who likes the assembly of heroes – warriors.

899. ॐ वीरायै नमः
ॐ वीरायै स्वाहा

Namaskar to the Valorous.

900. ॐ नैष्कर्म्यायै नमः
ॐ नैष्कर्म्यायै स्वाहा

Namaskar to the Mother, who is actionless.

901. ॐ नादरूपिण्यै नमः
ॐ नाद-रूपिण्यै स्वाहा

Namaskar to the Mother in the form of Nada Pranava AUM.

902. ॐ विज्ञानकलनायै नमः
ॐ विज्ञान-कलनायै स्वाहा

Namaskar to the Mother Causing perception, which blossoms in one's own being.

903. ॐ कल्यायै नमः
ॐ कल्यायै स्वाहा

Namaskar to the Skilful Mother.

904. ॐ विदग्धायै नमः
ॐ विदग्धायै स्वाहा

Namaskar to the Artful Mother.

905. ॐ बैन्दवासनायै नमः
ॐ बैन्दवासनायै स्वाहा

Namaskar to the Mother, who is seated on Baindava.

906. ॐ तत्त्वाधिकायै नमः
ॐ तत्व-अधिकायै स्वाहा

Namaskar to the Mother, who transcends the Categories.

907. ॐ तत्त्वमय्यै नमः
ॐ तत्त्व-मय्यै स्वाहा

Namaskar to the Mother Reality in itself.

908. ॐ तत्त्वमर्थस्वरूपिण्यै नमः
ॐ तन-त्वम्-अर्थ-स्वरूपिण्यै स्वाहा

Namaskar to the Mother in the manifestation of 'Word and Meaning'.

909. ॐ सामगानप्रियायै नमः
ॐ साम-गान-प्रियायै स्वाहा

Namaskar to the Mother, who is fond of the songs of Samaveda.

910. ॐ सौम्यायै नमः
ॐ सौम्यायै स्वाहा

Namaskar to the Benign Mother.

911. ॐ सदाशिवकुटुम्बिन्यै नमः
ॐ सदाशिव-कुटुम्बिन्यै स्वाहा

Namaskar to the Mother Family of Sadaṣhiva.

912. ॐ सव्यापसव्यमार्गस्थायै नमः
ॐ सव्य-अपसव्य-मार्गस्थायै स्वाहा

Namaskar to the Mother, who resides in the Right and Left paths.

913. ॐ सर्वापद्विनिवारिण्यै नमः
ॐ सर्वापत्-निवारिण्यै स्वाहा

Namaskar to the Mother, who removes all the misfortunes.

914. ॐ स्वस्थायै नमः
ॐ स्वस्थायै स्वाहा

Namaskar to the Svastha Mother - who abides in herself as Independent.

915. ॐ स्वभावमधुरायै नमः
ॐ स्वभाव-मधुरायै स्वाहा

Namaskar to the Mother, whose nature is Sweet.

916. ॐ धीरायै नमः
ॐ धीरायै स्वाहा

Namaskar to the knowledgable Mother.

917. ॐ धीरसमर्चितायै नमः
ॐ धीर-समर्चितायै स्वाहा

Namaskar to the Mother, who is adored by the wise.

918. ॐ चैतन्यार्घ्यसमाराध्यायै नमः
ॐ चैतन्य-अर्घ्य-समाराध्यायै स्वाहा

Namaskar to the Mother, who is adored with Consciousness as the oblation.

919. ॐ चैतन्यकुसुमप्रियायै नमः
ॐ चैतन्य-कुसुम-प्रियायै स्वाहा

Namaskar to the Mother, who is fond of Chaitanya flower of consciousness.

920. ॐ सदोदितायै नमः
ॐ सदा-उदितायै स्वाहा

Namaskar to the Mother, who is Ever Sublime.

921. ॐ सदातुष्टायै नमः
ॐ सदा-तुष्टायै स्वाहा

Namaskar to the Ever Contended Mother.

922. ॐ तरुणादित्यपाटलायै नमः
ॐ तरुण-आदित्य-पाटलायै स्वाहा

Namaskar to the Rosy Mother, who is like the Morning Sun.

923. ॐ दक्षिणादक्षिणाराध्यायै नमः
ॐ दक्षिणादक्षिण-आराध्यायै स्वाहा

Namaskar to the Mother, who is worshipped by 'Right and Left' hand.

924. ॐ दरस्मेरमुखाम्बुजायै नमः
ॐ दर-स्मेर-मुख-अम्बुजायै स्वाहा

Namaskar to the Lotus face of Mother, which is wreathed with sweet smiles.

925. ॐ कौलिनीकेवलायै नमः
ॐ कौलिनी-केवलायै स्वाहा

Namaskar to the Mother Kaulini, who is worshipped by the Kula-knowledge.

926. ॐ अनर्घ्यकैवल्यपददायिन्यै नमः
ॐ अनर्घ्य-कैवल्य-पद-दायिन्यै स्वाहा

Namaskar to the Mother, who gives the abode of priceless salvation.

927. ॐ स्तोत्रप्रियायै नमः
ॐ स्तोत्र-प्रियायै स्वाहा

Namaskar to the Mother, who is fond of praise.

928. ॐ स्तुतिमत्यै नमः
ॐ स्तुति-मत्यै स्वाहा

Namaskar to the Mother, who is the knowledge of Stuti – praises.

929. ॐ श्रुतिसंस्तुतवैभवायै नमः
ॐ श्रुति-संस्तुत-वैभवायै स्वाहा

Namaskar to the Mother, whose Glory is celebrated in the scriptures.

930. ॐ मनस्विन्यै नमः
ॐ मनस्विन्यै स्वाहा

Namaskar to the Intelligent Mother.

931. ॐ मानवत्यै नमः
ॐ मानवत्यै स्वाहा

Namaskar to the Mother, whose mind is elevated.

932. ॐ महेश्यै नमः
ॐ महेश्यै स्वाहा

Namaskar to the Mother Maheshi – spouse of Mahesha.

933. ॐ मङ्गलाकृत्ये नमः
ॐ मङ्गल-आकृत्यै स्वाहा

Namaskar to the Beneficial appearance of the Mother.

934. ॐ विश्वमात्रे नमः
ॐ विश्व-मात्रे स्वाहा

Namaskar to the Universal Mother.

935. ॐ जगद्धात्र्यै नमः
ॐ जगत्-दात्र्यै स्वाहा

Namaskar to the World Supporting Mother.

936. ॐ विशालाक्ष्यै नमः
ॐ विशालाक्ष्यै स्वाहा

Namaskar to the Large-eyed Mother.

937. ॐ विरागिण्यै नमः
ॐ विरागिण्यै स्वाहा

Namaskar to the Dispassionate Mother.

938. ॐ प्रगल्भायै नमः
ॐ प्रगल्भायै स्वाहा

Namaskar to the Mother Strength.

939. ॐ परमोदारायै नमः
ॐ परमोदारायै स्वाहा

Namaskar to the Supremely generous Mother.

940. ॐ परमोदायै नमः
ॐ परमोदायै स्वाहा

Namaskar to the Supremely delightful Mother.

941. ॐ मनोमय्यै नमः
ॐ मनोमय्यै स्वाहा

Namaskar to the Mother Mind.

942. ॐ व्योमकेश्यै नमः
ॐ व्योम-केश्यै स्वाहा

Namaskar to the hair of the Mother, which is manifest in ether.

943. ॐ विमानस्थायै नमः
ॐ विमानस्थायै स्वाहा

Namaskar to the Mother, who resides in the celestial chariot.

944. ॐ वज्रिण्यै नमः
ॐ वज्रिण्यै स्वाहा

Namaskar to the Vajrini Mother–Thunderbolt.

945. ॐ वामकेश्वर्यै नमः
ॐ वामकेश्वर्यै स्वाहा

Namaskar to the Vamakeshvari Mother – the presiding deity of Creation.

946. ॐ पञ्चयज्ञप्रियायै नमः
ॐ पञ्च-यज्ञ-प्रियायै स्वाहा

Namaskar to the Mother, who is fond of the five Sacrifices.

947. ॐ पञ्चप्रेतमञ्चाधिशायिन्यै नमः
ॐ पञ्च-प्रेत-मञ्च-अधिशायिन्यै स्वाहा

Namaskar to the Mother, who rests upon a couch formed of five corpses.

948. ॐ पञ्चम्यै नमः
ॐ पञ्चम्यै स्वाहा

Namaskar to the Mother Panchami – bliss of the fifth Digit of moon.

949. ॐ पञ्चभूतेश्यै नमः
ॐ पञ्च-भूतेश्यै स्वाहा

Namaskar to the Mother, who is the Ruler of five elements.

950. ॐ पञ्चसङ्खयोपचारिण्यै नमः
ॐ पञ्च-सङ्खयोपचारिण्यै स्वाहा

Namaskar to the Mother, who is worshipped with five objects.

951. ॐ शाश्वत्यै नमः
ॐ शाश्वत्यै स्वाहा

Namaskar to the Eternal Mother.

952. ॐ शाश्वतैश्वर्यायै नमः
ॐ शाश्वत-ऐश्वर्यायै स्वाहा

Namaskar to the Mother, who possesses eternal dominion.

953. ॐ शर्मदायै नमः
ॐ शर्मदायै स्वाहा

Namaskar to the Mother Happiness.

954. ॐ शम्भुमोहिन्यै नमः
ॐ शम्भु-मोहिन्यै स्वाहा

Namaskar to the Mother, who bewilders Shambu.

955. ॐ धरायै नमः
ॐ धरायै स्वाहा

Namaskar to the Mother Earth.

956. ॐ धरसुतायै नमः
ॐ धर-सुतायै स्वाहा

Namaskar to the Mother - Himavan's daughter.

957. ॐ धन्यायै नमः
ॐ धन्यायै स्वाहा

Namaskar to the Mother Fortune.

958. ॐ धर्मिण्यै नमः
ॐ धर्मिण्यै स्वाहा

Namaskar to the Righteous Mother.

959. ॐ धर्मवर्धिन्यै नमः
ॐ धर्म-वर्धिन्यै स्वाहा

Namaskar to the Mother, who is the Increaser of righteousness.

960. ॐ लोकातीतायै नमः
ॐ लोकातीतायै स्वाहा

Namaskar to the Mother who Transcends the worlds.

961. ॐ गुणातीतायै नमः
ॐ गुणातीतायै स्वाहा

Namaskar to the Mother, who is beyond attributes.

962. ॐ सर्वातीतायै नमः
ॐ सर्वातीतायै स्वाहा

Namaskar to the All transcending Mother.

963. ॐ शमात्मिकायै नमः
ॐ शमात्मिकायै स्वाहा

Namaskar to the Mother Tranquility.

964. ॐ बन्धूककुसुमप्रख्यायै नमः
ॐ बन्धूक-कुसुम-प्रख्यायै स्वाहा

Namaskar to the Mother, who resembles the Bhanduka flower.

965. ॐ बालायै नमः
ॐ बालायै स्वाहा

Namaskar to the Mother Bala – girl.

966. ॐ लीलाविनोदिन्यै नमः

ॐ लीला-विनोदिन्यै स्वाहा

Namaskar to the Mother, who takes pleasure is amusement.

967. ॐ सुमुङ्गल्यै नमः

ॐ सुमङ्गल्यै स्वाहा

Namaskar to the Supremely auspicious Mother.

968. ॐ सुखकर्यै नमः

ॐ सुख-कर्यै स्वाहा

Namaskar to the Mother, who gives happiness.

969. ॐ सुवेषाढ्यायै नमः

ॐ सुवेषाढ्यायै स्वाहा

Namaskar to the Mother, who is fittingly decked with beautiful raiments.

970. ॐ सुवासिन्यै नमः

ॐ सुवासिन्यै स्वाहा

Namaskar to the Ever married Mother.

971. ॐ सुवासिन्यर्चनप्रीतायै नमः

ॐ सुवासिनी-अर्चन-प्रीतायै स्वाहा

Namaskar to the Mother, who is pleased by the adoration of married women.

972. ॐ आशोभनायै नमः

ॐ आशोभनायै स्वाहा

Namaskar to the Ever beautiful Mother.

973. ॐ शुद्धमानसायै नमः

ॐ शुद्ध-मानसायै स्वाहा

Namaskar to the Pure-minded Mother.

974. ॐ बिन्दुतर्पणसन्तुष्टायै नमः

ॐ बिन्दु-तर्पण-सन्तुष्टायै स्वाहा

Namaskar to the Mother, who is pleased by offerings in the Bindu.

975. ॐ पूर्वजायै नमः
ॐ पूर्वजायै स्वाहा

Namaskar to the First-born Mother.

976. ॐ त्रिपुराम्बिकायै नमः
ॐ त्रिपुराम्बिकायै स्वाहा

Namaskar to the Mother Tripurambika - the eighth chakra of Sri Yantra.

977. ॐ दशमुद्रासमाराध्यायै नमः
ॐ दश-मुद्रा-सम-आराध्यायै स्वाहा

Namaskar to the Mother, who is adored with ten Mudras - finger positions.

978. ॐ त्रिपुराश्रीवशंकर्यै नमः
ॐ त्रिपुराश्री-वशंकर्यै स्वाहा

Namaskar to the Ruling Mother Tripura.

979. ॐ ज्ञानमुद्रायै नमः
ॐ ज्ञान-मुद्रायै स्वाहा

Namaskar to the Mother Jnanamudra – a mudra by joining the tips of the thumb and forefinger.

980. ॐ ज्ञानगम्यायै नमः
ॐ ज्ञानगम्यायै स्वाहा

Namaskar to the Mother, who is attained by Knowledge.

981. ॐ ज्ञानज्ञेयस्वरूपिण्यै नमः
ॐ ज्ञान-ज्ञेय-स्वरूपिण्यै स्वाहा

Namaskar to the Mother manifest in Knowledge and knowing.

982. ॐ योनिमुद्रायै नमः
ॐ योनि-मुद्रायै स्वाहा

Namaskar to the Mother Yonimudra – the finger position of womb.

983. ॐ त्रिखण्डेश्यै नमः
ॐ त्रिखण्डेश्यै स्वाहा

Namaskar to the Ruling Mother of Trikhanda – the three kutas of Panchadashi Mantra.

984. ॐ त्रिगुणायै नमः
ॐ त्रिगुणायै स्वाहा

Namaskar to the mother Triguna – a composition of three qualities.

985. ॐ अम्बायै नमः
ॐ अम्बायै स्वाहा

Namaskar to the Mother Amba – Universal Mother.

986. ॐ त्रिकोणगायै नमः
ॐ त्रिकोणगायै स्वाहा

Namaskar to the Mother, who resides in the triangle.

987. ॐ अनघायै नमः
ॐ अनघायै स्वाहा

Namaskar to the Sinless Mother.

988. ॐ अदभुतचारित्रायै नमः
ॐ अदभुत-चारित्रायै स्वाहा

Namaskar to the Mother, whose deeds are wonderful.

989. ॐ वाञ्छितार्थप्रदायिन्यै नमः
ॐ वाञ्छित-अर्थ-प्रदायिन्यै स्वाहा

Namaskar to the Bestowing Mother of the desired objects.

990. ॐ अभ्यासातिशयज्ञातायै नमः
ॐ अभ्यास-अतिशय-ज्ञातायै स्वाहा

Namaskar to the Mother, who is known through constant devotion.

991. ॐ षडध्वातीतरूपिण्यै नमः
ॐ षडध्वातीत्-रूपिण्यै स्वाहा

Namaskar to the Mother, who transcends the form of six modes of devotion.

992. ॐ अव्याजकरुणामूर्तये नमः
ॐ अव्याज-करुणा-मूर्तये स्वाहा

Namaskar to the Compassionate Mother, who is without partiality.

993. ॐ अज्ञानध्वान्तदीपिकायै नमः
ॐ अज्ञान-ध्वान्त-दीपिकायै स्वाहा

Namaskar to the Mother Lamp, that dispells the darkness of ignorance.

994. ॐ आबालगोपविदितायै नमः
ॐ आबाल-गोप-विदितायै स्वाहा

Namaskar to the Mother, who is known to Children and Cowherds.

995. ॐ सर्वानुल्लङ्घ्यशासनायै नमः
ॐ सर्व-अनुल्लङ्घ्य-शासनायै स्वाहा

Namaskar to the Mother, whose Commands are never ignored.

996. ॐ श्रीचक्रराजनिलयायै नमः
ॐ श्री-चक्र-राज-निलयायै स्वाहा

Namaskar to the Mother, whose abode is Srichakra.

997. ॐ श्रीमत्त्रिपुरसुन्दर्यै नमः
ॐ श्रीमत्-त्रिपुर-सुन्दर्यै स्वाहा

Namaskar to the Mother Sri Tripura Sundari.

998. ॐ श्रीशिवायै नमः
ॐ श्री-शिवायै स्वाहा

Namaskar to the Mother Sri Shiva.

999. ॐ शिवशक्त्यैक्यरूपिण्यै नमः
ॐ शिव-शक्ति-एक्य-रूपिण्यै स्वाहा

Namaskar to the Mother, who is the only Union of Shiva and Shakti.

1000. ॐ ललिताम्बिकायै नमः
ॐ ललिताम्बिकायै स्वाहा

Namaskar to the Mother Lalita Ambika – the most conspicuously beautiful Mother.

प्रार्थना

त्वां व्यापिनीति सुमना इति कुण्डलीति
त्वां कामिनीति कमलेति कलावततीति।
त्वां मालिनीति ललितेत्यपराजितेति
देवि! स्तुवन्ति विजयेति जयेत्युमेति।

O Supreme Sovereign Lalita Devi! You are manifest in all the creation *(jada-chaitana)*, non-conscious and conscious being. You are the embodiment of supreme 'Mana' - mental faculty and verily present in the Kundalini Shakti the Serpent coil energy of Shaktas. You are the Kamini - the will power adorned with all the 'Kalas' - digital power and You are Kamala - the being of 'Sankocha-Vikas'. You are Malini - the manifestation of Varnamala - garland of syllables. None equals you, O Mother! You are Vijaya - vanquisher of all. You are Jaya - ever victorious. The devotees bow to you with Stuti - adoration with these specific names.

शिवस्त्वं शक्तिस्त्वं त्वमसि समया त्वं समयिनी
त्वमात्मा त्वं दीक्षा त्वमयमणिमादिर्गुणगणः।
अविद्या त्वं विद्या त्वंमसि निखिलं त्वं किमपरं
प्रथक्तत्वं त्वत्तो भगवति न वीक्षामहे इमे।।

O Divine Bhagvati! You are Supreme 'Shiva'. You are 'Shakti'. You are 'Samaya' - the concept and principle of the Triadic form. Verily, You are 'Samayini' - the instrument and practice of the Triadic system. You are Atman - the Supreme Self. You are Diksha - the initiation You are manifest in the Ashta-Siddhis like Anima etc., and exist in Triple Gunas - nature. Verily, You are manifest in Avidya, but You are Vidya-Great and Supreme knowledge, You are manifest everywhere and ever existent. You are the Possessor of all. Nothing but You alone exist, as we realize, feel and see.

अथोत्तरभाग फलश्रुतिः

Uttarbhaga - Epilogue and Achievement of merits

1. इत्येतन्नामसाहस्त्रं कथितं ते घटोद्भव।
रहस्यानां रहस्यं च ललिताप्रीतिदायकम॥

O Pot born Agastya! I have narrated you the most mysterious and highly occult Sahasranama of one thousand attributes, very dear to Sri Lalita Devi.

2. अनेन सदृशं स्तोत्रं न भूतं न भविष्यति।
सर्वरोगप्रशमनं सर्वसम्पत्प्रवर्धनम्॥

No other Sahasranama can be compared either in the past or in future, with it. It is, verily, the destroyer of all the diseases and the granter of the extension of all kinds of wealth.

3. सर्वापमृत्युशमनं कालमृत्युनिवारणम्।
सर्वज्वरार्तिशमनं दीर्घायुष्यप्रदायकम्॥

It subsides all the untimely deaths and wards off timely death. It subsides all sorts of ailments of fever and grants longevity to the devotees.

4. पुत्रप्रदमपुत्राणां पुरुषार्थप्रदायकम्।
इदं विशेषाच्छ्रीदेव्याः स्तोत्रं प्रीतिविधायकम्॥

Gives blessings of son to those, who have no son in their progeny, and blesses with all the Purusharthas, viz. dharma, artha, kama, moksha. All these merits are possible to him alone, who endearlingly recite the stotram with enthusiasm of Sri Devi.

5 जपेन्नित्यं प्रयत्नेन ललितोपास्तितत्परः।
प्रातः स्नात्वा विधानेन सन्ध्याकर्म समाप्य च॥

With firm determination and concentration, you should perform 'japam' in the Upasana of Sri Lalita, after taking a morning bath, and do 'sandhya-karma' - twilight duties methodically.

6. पूजागृहं ततो गत्वा चक्रराजं समर्चयेत्।
विद्या जपेत् सहस्त्रं वा त्रिशतं शतमेव वा॥

Then one should go to the Sanctum-Sanctorum and worship the Chakraraja. Japam of Sri Vidya should be performed a thousand or three hundred or a hundred times.

7. रहस्यनामसहस्रमिदं पश्चात् पठेन्नरः ।
जन्ममध्ये सकृच्चापि य एवं पठते सुधीः ।।

Then one should recite this highly occult Sahasranama. If any learned devotee recites only once, during his life time; he also achieves the great merits.

8. तस्य पुण्यफलं वक्ष्ये शृणु त्वं कुम्भसम्भव ।
गङ्गादिसर्वतीर्थेषु यः स्नायात्कोटिजन्मसु ।।

O Pot-born Agastya! Listen to his merits. He who recites this Sahasranama, gets more merits than who takes holy dip in the Ganga and other pilgrimages in millions of births.

9. कोटिलिङ्गप्रतिष्ठां च यः कुर्यादविमुक्तके ।
कुरुक्षेत्रे तु यो दद्यात्कोटिवारं रविग्रहे ।।

Or who may install the millions of 'Lingam', or who may offer the presents to the deserved persons a million times at the time of Solar eclipse...,

10. कोटिसौवर्णभाराणां श्रोत्रियेषु द्विजन्मसु ।
यः कोटिं हयमेधानामाहरेद् गाङ्गरोघसि ।।

In the form of golden sovereigns to the Brahmins, well experts in Shruti the Vedas who may also perform the 'anushtanam' of millions of Ashva medha Yajnas – horse sacrifices on the bank of the holy river Ganga.

11. आचरेत्कूपकोटीर्यो निर्जलेमरुभूतले ।
दुर्भिक्षे यः प्रतिदिनं कोटिब्राह्मणभोजनम् ।।

Or whosoever digs millions of wells at the drought hit areas of deserts or feeds the millions of hunger stricken Brahmans daily, at the time of famine.

12. श्रद्धया परया कुर्यात्सहस्रपरिवत्सरान् ।
तत्पुण्यं कोटिगुणितं लमेत् पुण्यमनुत्तमम् ।।

The man who-so-ever recites this Sahasranama with faith and devotion, gets millions of times more merits than doing the other Sadhanas...,

13. रहस्यानामसाहस्रे नाम्नोऽप्येकस्य कीर्तनात् ।
रहस्यनामसाहस्रे नामैकमपि यः पठेत् ।।

Who performs the Kirtanam of only single name of this occult thousand names, or does 'Patham' of a single name alone, of this Sahasranama...,

14. तस्य पापानि नश्यन्ति महान्त्यपि न संशयः ।
नित्यकर्माननुष्ठानान्निषिद्धकरणादपि ।।

His great sins get washed off. There is no doubt about it. All the sins afflicted due to non-performance of 'nitya-karma' – regular duties and by performing the unwanted action get destroyed...

15. यत्पापं जायते पुंसां तत्सर्वं नश्यति ध्रुवम् ।
बहुनात्र किमुक्तेन शृणु त्वं कुम्भसम्भव ।।

There is no need to tell you about all of the merits. All the acquired sins are destroyed with certainity. So listen to it with confidence, you the 'Pot-born'-Agastya.

16. अत्रैकनाम्नो या शक्तिः पातकानां निवर्तने ।
तन्निवर्त्यमघं कर्तुं नालं लोकाश्चतुर्दश ।।

All the fourteen lokas have not got so much potency to ward off the sins, as it is potent in the single name of this Sahasranama.

17. यस्त्यक्त्वा नामसाहस्रं पापहानिमभीप्सति ।
स हि शीतनिवृत्यर्थं हिमशैलं निषेवते ।।

Any person who wants to wash off the sins , through other measures save this Sahasranama, he acts the way like one, who sits on the ice slab, to get rid of the severe cold.

18. भक्तो यः कीर्तयेन्नित्यमिदं नामसहस्रकम् ।
तस्मै श्रीललितादेवी प्रीताभीष्टं प्रयच्छति ।।

Sri Lalita Devi bestows upon him all the best as desired by the devotee who recites the 'Kirtanam' of this Sahasranam constantly.

19. अकीर्तयन्निदं स्तोत्रं कथं भक्तो भविष्यति ।
नित्यं सङ्कीर्तनाशक्तः कीर्तयेत्पुण्यवासरे ।।

How can one be a devotee of Sri Lalita Devi, without reciting the 'Kirtanam' of this Stotram? Now, whosoever may be unable to do the 'Kirtanam' regularly, must do it on the sacred occasions.

20. संक्रान्तौ विषुवे चैव स्वजन्मत्रितयेऽयने।
नवम्यां वा चतुर्दश्यां सितायां शुक्रवासरे।।

One must do the 'Kirtanam' on the occasion of the 'Vishuva-Sankranti' – the first portion of 'Mesha and Tula Rashi', where the Sun enters into the Vishuva point of aeries and libra of the Zodiac signs; or on the three birth-days or on ninth and fourteenth tithi of the lunar fortnight and on Fridays.

21. कीर्तयेन्नामसाहस्रं पौर्णमास्यां विशेषतः।
पौर्णमास्यां चन्द्रबिम्बे ध्यात्वा श्रीललिताम्बिकाम्।।

On the Purnima – the full moon night, the devotee must specially with care recite Sahasranama. He should meditate upon the moon as the very being of Sri Lalitambika and perform 'Kirtanam' of this sacred Sahasranama.

22. पञ्चोपचारैः सम्पूज्य पठेन्नामसहस्रकम्।
सर्वे रोगाः प्रणवृयन्ति दीर्घमायुश्च विन्दति।।

It should be read properly with its limbs of 'Panchopchara', with which all the ailments come to an end and the devotee is graced with the longevity.

23. अयमायुष्करो नाम प्रयोगः कल्पचोदितः।
ज्वरार्तं शिरसि स्पृष्ट्वा पठेन्नामसहस्रकम्।।

The 'Prayoga' – implementation of this sacred Patham – recitation is for rejuvenation of life and the ailing person with fever must be touched by head and recite the Sahasranama accordingly.

24. तत्क्षणात्प्रशमं याति शिरस्तोदो ज्वरोऽपि च।
सर्वव्याधिनिवृत्त्यर्थं स्पृष्ट्वा भस्म जपेदिदम्।।

Instantly the fever subsides and the head-ache gets cured. All the diseases get cured when one tonches the head with sacred ashes after its proper recitation.

26. तद्भस्मधारणादेव नश्यन्ति व्याधयः क्षणात्।
जलं सम्मन्त्र्य कुम्भस्थं नामसाहस्रतो मुने।।

All the diseases disappear, when the Bhasma sacred ashes are applied on the ailing person. The water is to be sanctified in the 'Kumbham' pot while reciting the Sahasranama. O Muni

26. अभिषिञ्चेन्द्ग्रहस्तान् ग्रहा नश्यन्ति तत्क्षणात् ।
सुधासागरमध्यस्थां ध्यात्वा श्रीललिताम्बिकाम् ।।

All the evil influences are warded off instantaneously, when sprinkled with the sanctified water. Sri Lalitambika should be meditated upon as manifested amidst in the ocean of nectar.

27. यः पठेन्नामसाहस्रं विषं तस्य विनश्यति ।
वन्ध्यानां पुत्रलाभाय नामसाहस्रमन्त्रितम् ।।

All kinds of venoms get neutralized, when the Sahasranama is recited; and the barren woman gives birth to a son, with the efficiency of this mantra...,

28. नवनीतं प्रदद्यात्तु पुत्रलाभो भवेद् ध्रुवम् ।
देव्याः पाशेन सम्बद्धामाकृष्टामङ्कुशेन च ।।

When the butter is sanctified with this Sahasranama and offered to the woman for giving birth to a sin. With the noose and goad of the Devi, the woman gets attracted with...,

29. ध्यात्वाभीष्टां स्त्रियं रात्रौ जपेन्नामसहस्रकम् ।
आयाति स्वसमीपं सा यद्यप्यन्त पुरं गता ।।

The person, when japam of Sahasranama is performed during night. She comes herself before the person, even if she happens to be in the women's apartment.

30. राजाकर्षणकामश्चेद् राजावसथदिङ्मुखः ।
त्रिरात्रं यः पठेदेतच्छ्रीदेवीध्यानतत्परः ।।

A king can make another king surrender to his sovereignty within three nights, if the recitation of this Sahasranama is done with concentration towards the direction, his kingdom is situated.

31. स राजा पारवश्येन तुरङ्गं वा मतङ्गजम् ।
आरुह्यायाति निकटं दासवत् प्रणिपत्याच ।।

Thus the king submits to his sovereignty and comes riding on horses along with elephants, and bows down like a slave.

32. तस्मै राज्यं च कोशं च ददात्येव वशं गतः ।
रहस्यनामसाहस्रं यः कीर्तयति नित्यशः ।।

Under this influence, he gives him the kingdom and treasure house whosoever performs the kirtanam of this occult Sahasranama regularly...,

33. तन्मुखालोकमात्रेण मुह्येल्लोकत्रयं मुने ।
यस्त्विदं नामसाहस्रं सकृत् पठति भक्तिमान् ।।

O Muni! All this triple world get bewitched while having a look on his face. Whosoever recites once only the Sahasranama....,

34. तस्य ये शत्रवस्तेषां निहन्ता शरभेश्वरः ।
यो वाभिचारं कुरुते नाम साहस्रपाठके ।।

Sharbheshvara – the lord of wild beast kills and his enemies are subdued. Whatsoever applies witchcraft to the devotee of this Sahasranama...,

35. निवर्त्य तत्क्रियां हन्यात्त वै प्रत्यङ्गिरास्स्वयम् ।
ये क्रूरदृष्टया वीक्षन्ते नाम साहस्रपाठकमू ।।

His influence of magic is put to an end; also who sees with cruel eye at the devotee of Sahasranama...,

36. तनन्धान्कुरुते क्षिप्रं स्वयं मार्ताण्डभैरवः ।
धन यो हरते चौरोर्नामिसाहस्रजापिनः ।।

The 'Martanda Bhairava' himself makes them blind immediately. To the 'Japin' – the devotee of this Sahasranama, if the thief makes theft of his wealth....,

37. यत्र कुत्र स्थितं वापि क्षेत्रपालो निहन्ति तम् ।
विद्यासु कुरुते वादं यो विद्वान्नामजापिनः ।।

Wherever, he may be hidden, the Kshetrapala kills him there and then, & whosoever be the learned but refutes the 'Nama-japin' – the devotee who perform the japam of Sahasranama...,

38. तस्य वाक्स्तम्भनं सद्यः करोति नकुलेश्वरी ।
यो राजा कुरुते वैरं नामसाहस्रजापिना ।।

His power of speech is being blocked for ever, by the Nakuleshvari. The king who keeps enmity with the 'Nama-japin'....,

39. चतुरङगबलं तस्य दण्डिनी संहरेत् स्वयम् ।
यः पठेन्नामसाहस्रं षण्मासं भक्तिसंयुतः ।।

To him the Dandini destroys herself his chaturange - four limbed force. He who recites the Namasahasra with keen devotion for six months......,

40. लक्ष्मीश्चाञ्चल्यरहिता सदा तिष्ठति तद्गृहे।
मासमेकं प्रतिदिनं त्रिवारं यः पठेन्नरः।।

There, Lakshmi in wealth form rests in his house permanently without any disturbance. He who recites it regularly for a month, thrice a day...,

41. भारती तस्य जिस्वाग्रे रङ्गे नृत्यति नित्यशः।
यस्त्वेकवारं पठति पक्षमात्रमतन्द्रितः।।

'Bharati' in the form of Sarasvati rests at the tip of his tongue, playing the tune of action always. He who performs the Patham only once in a fortnight with dedication and control of senses...,

42. मुह्यन्ति कामवश्यगा मृगाक्ष्यस्तस्य वीक्षणात्।
यः पठेन्नामसाहस्त्रं जन्ममध्ये सकृन्तरः।।

The beautiful women having the eyes like deer gets attracted to him, only if he glances at them. He who recites only once the 'patham' of this Sahasranama, during his life span...,

43. तदृष्टिगोचराः सर्वे मुच्यन्ते सर्वकिल्बषैः।।
यो वेत्ति नामसाहस्त्रं तस्मै देयं द्विजन्मने।।

He becomes instrumental in making them free from the bondages of all troubles, merely with his glances. The Brahman who is proficient in this occult Sahasranama, must be presented with...,

44. अन्नं वस्त्रं धनं धान्यं नान्येभ्यस्तु कदाचन।
श्रीमन्त्रराजं यो वेत्ति श्रीचक्रं यः समर्चति।।

Food, clothing, wealth, crops and not to present to any other person in any way and form. He who is proficient in the niceties of Sri Mantraraja and he who worships properly the Sri Chakra...,

45. यः कीर्तयति नामानि तं सत्पात्रं विदुर्बुधाः।
तस्मै देयं प्रयत्नेन श्रीदेवीप्रीतिमिच्छता।।

The men with wisdom consider him alone the 'Satpatra' – genuine person to receive such gifts, who makes the 'Kirtanam' of the sacred names. Those who are attached with the glory of Sri Devi, must make the offerings to such a genuine person with efforts.

46. न कीर्तयति नामनि मन्त्रराजं न वेत्ति यः।
पशुतुल्यः स विज्ञेयस्तस्मै दत्तं निरर्थकम्।।

He who does not recite the sacred names or does not know the niceties of Mantraraja, he is just like a beast. The gift presented to him goes all waste.

47. परीक्ष्य विद्याविदुषस्तेभ्यो दद्याद्विचक्षणः।
श्रीमन्त्रराजसदृशो यथा मन्त्रो न विद्यते।।

A wise man must examine the person's proficiency in Sri Vidya, before presenting him the donations. No mantra equals the Sri Mantra raja.

48. देवता ललितातुल्या यथा नास्ति घटओद्भव।
रहस्यनामसाहस्रतुल्या नास्ति तथा स्तुतिः।।

O Gatodbhava – 'Pot-born' Agastya! As no devata stands equal before Sri Lalita, so no 'Stuti' can equal the highly occult Sahasranama.

49. लिखित्वा पुस्तके यस्तु नामसाहस्रमुत्तमम्।
समर्चयेत् सदा भक्त्या तस्य तुष्यति सुन्दरी।।

He who writes this Supreme Sahasranama in the book form, and will make obeisance to it with devotion, on him the Lalita Sundari gets ever satisfied.

50. बहुनात्र किमुक्तेन शृणु त्वं कुम्भसम्भव।
नानेन सदृशं स्तोत्रं सर्वतन्त्रेषु दृश्यते।।

There is no need to tell more and more of the merits earned by reciting the Sahsranama. O Kumbha-Sambhava Agastya! Of all the Tantras, there is no such potent stotram, as it is, verily.

51. तस्मादुपासको नित्यं कीर्तयेदिदमादरात्।
एभिर्नामसहस्रैस्तु श्रीचक्रं योऽर्चयेत्सकृत्।।

Therefore, the Upasaka must make the 'kirtaman' with great reverence. He who makes 'archana' uttering these thousand names upon Sri Chakra...,

52. पद्मैर्वा तुलसीपुष्पैः कल्हारैर्वा कदम्बकैः।
चम्पकैर्जातिकुसुमैः मल्लिकाकरवीरकैः।।

With the variety of lotus, Tulasi, Kalhara, Kadambaka, Champaka, Jati, Mallika, Karavira.,

53. उत्पलैर्बिल्वपत्रैर्वा कुन्दकेसरपाटलैः ।
अन्यैः सुगन्धिकुसुमैः केतकीमाधवीमुखैः ।।

Utpala, Bilva - leaves, Kunda-Kesara, Patala and other fragrant flowers like Ketaki, Madhavi, etc..,

54. तस्य पुण्यफलं वक्तुं न शक्नोति महेश्वरः ।
सा वेत्ति ललितादेवी स्वचक्रार्चनजं फलम् ।।

His 'punya-phalam' – fruits of Supreme merit can not even be enumerated by Maheshvara. Lalita Devi alone knows the merits of doing her 'archana' in the Chakraraja.

55. अन्ये कथं विजानीयुर्ब्रह्माद्याः स्वल्पमेधसः ।
प्रतिमासं पौर्णमास्यामेभिर्नामसहस्रकैः ।।

How able with lesser intellect are to explain the merits like Brahma and host of other Devas? He who recites every month on the Purnima the full moon digit day this Sahasranama..

56. रात्रौ यश्चक्रराजस्थामर्चयेत् परदेवताम् ।
स एव ललितारूपस्तद्रूपा ललिता स्वयम् ।।

Of Para Shakti upon the Chakraraja during night, he becomes identical with Sri Lalita, and Lalita Devi becomes manifest in him.

57. न तयोर्विद्यते भेदो भेदकृत् पापकृदभवेत् ।
महानवम्यां यो भक्तः श्रीदेवीं चक्रमध्यगाम् ।।

There is no differentiation between the two, he who sees difference in them is subjected to sin. The devotee, who worships at the centre of the Chakra of Sri Devi on the Mahanavami day...,

58. अर्चयेन्नामसाहस्रैस्तस्य मुक्तिः करे स्थिता ।
यस्तु नामसहस्रेण शुक्रवारे समर्चयेत् ।।

With this Sahasranama, he is bestowed with Moksha, which is easily accessible to him. He who makes proper 'archana' of this Sahasranama on Fridays....

59. चक्रराजे महादेवी तस्य पुण्यफलं शृणु ।
सर्वान् कामानावाप्येह सर्वसौभाग्यसंयुतः ।।

Before the Chakraraja of Maha Devi; you listen to those merits accrued by it. The devotee is filled with grace and all fortune he achieves all the goals of his life.

60. पुत्रपौत्रादिसंयुक्तो भुक्त्वा भोगान् यथेप्सितान् ।
अन्ते श्रीललितादेव्या सायुज्यमतिदुर्लभम् ।।

He is blessed with sons and grandsons. He reaps the desired fruits of his merits and lastly, the devotee merges with Sri Lalita Devi. which is otherwise. difficult to attain

61. प्रार्थनीयं शिवाद्यैश्च प्राप्नोत्येव न संशयः ।
यः सहस्रं ब्राह्मणानामेभिर्नामसहस्रकैः ।।

He gets this status, which is even desired by Lord Shiva and others. He who feeds the thousand Brahmans reciting these sacred names...,

62. समर्च्य भोजयेद्भक्त्या पायसाऽपूपषड्रसैः ।
तस्मै प्रीणाति ललिता स्वसाम्राज्यं प्रयच्छति ।।

With 'payasam', 'apupam' and 'shadrasam' with devotion, to him Lalita Devi endearingly gives her own Sovereignty.

63. न तस्य दुर्लभं वस्तु त्रिषु लोकेषु विद्यते ।
निष्कामः कीर्तयेद्यस्तु नामसाहस्रमुत्तमम् ।।

He falls nothing short of in all the three worlds. He who performs the 'kirtanam' with detachment...,

64. ब्रह्मज्ञानमवाप्नोति येन मुच्येत बन्धनात् ।
धनार्थी धनमाप्नोति यशोऽर्थी चाप्नुयाद्यशः ।।

Attains the Brahmajnanam, which makes a man free from bondage. He who is desirous of wealth gets wealth in abundance, and one achieves higher 'name and fame', when one desires such things.

65. विद्यार्थी चाप्नुयाद् विद्यां नामसाहस्रकीर्तनात् ।
नानेन सदृशं स्तोत्रं भोगमोक्षप्रदं मुने ।।

With the efficacy of 'nama-kirtanam', a scholar attains higher learning. O Muni! There is no parallel Stotram, which blesses with 'Bhoga' – fulfilments and 'Moksha' – the final beautitude.

66. कीर्तनीयमिदं तस्माद् भोगमोक्षार्थिभिनरैः ।
चतुराश्रमनिष्ठैश्च कीर्तनीयमिदं सदा ।।

Those who long for 'Bhoga' and 'Moksha', should therefore, do the 'Kirtanam' of this Sahasranama. Belonging to the four 'ashramas' - 'brahamacharya, grihstha, Vanparastha and Sannyas' must also recite the Kirtanam with dedication.

67 स्वधर्मसमनुष्ठानवैकल्यपरिपूर्तये ।
कलौ पापैकबहुले धर्मानुष्ठानवर्जिते ।।

During this Kali-yuga, where there is no end to sins; and people are devoid of 'Dharma'-Duty and 'Anushthanam' - proper religious exercise in rituals, only the Anushtanam of this Sahasranama will supplement in their path of virtue.

68. नामानुकीर्तनं भुक्त्वा नृणां नान्यत् परायणम् ।
लौकिकाद् वचनान्मुख्यं विष्णुनामानुकीर्तनम् ।।

Without 'Namakirtanam', there is no proper remedy in this dark era of Kaliyuga. Vishnu Sahasranama is chief and superior to other local hymns in the Kirtanam.

69 विष्णुनामसहस्राच्च शिवनामैकमुत्तमम् ।
शिवनामसहस्राच्च देव्या नामैकमुत्तमम् ।।

Singular name of Shiva alone excels the Vishnusahasranama and the name of Devi is far superior to the thousand names of Shiva alone.

70. देवीनामसहस्राणि कोटिशः सन्ति कुम्भज ।
तेषु मुख्यं दशविधं नामसाहस्रमुच्येतै ।।

O Kumbhaja-Agastya! "Verily, there exist the millions of Devi Sahasranamas. Of them, the supreme one happens to be Dashavidham Namasahasram...,

71 गङ्गा भवानी गायत्री काली लक्ष्मीस्सरस्वती ।
राजराजेश्वरी बाला श्यामला ललिता दश ।।

Which serially are the Ganga, Bhavani, Gayatri, Kali, Lakshmi , Sarasvati, Rajarajeshvari, Bala, Shyamala and Lalita all ten in number.

72. रहस्यानामसाहस्रमिदं शस्तं दशस्वपि ।
तस्मात् सङ्कीर्तयेन्नित्यं कलिदोषनिवृत्तये ।।

Of these 'Dashavidha Sahasranamas', this Rahasyanama Sahasram excels in every aspect. To remove the stains of sins of the Kaliyuga, you should invariably perform the 'Namakirtanam' of this highly occult Sahasranama.

73. मुख्यं श्रीमातृनामेति न जानन्ति विमोहिताः ।
विष्णुनामपराः केचिच्छिवनामपराः परे ।।

Deluded persons are not conversant with the name of Sri Mata as being the Chief one. Among them, some consider the name of Vishnu and others the name of Shiva Superior to in the transcendental nature.

74. न कश्चिदपि लोकेषु ललितानामतत्परः ।
येनान्यदेवतानाम कीर्तितं जन्मकोटिषु ।।

There is no, of course, any other name superior to the name of sacred Lalita in all the worlds. Whosoever has performed the kirtanam of other Devatas in millions of births...,

75. तस्यैव भवतिश्रद्धा श्रीदेवीनामकीर्तने ।
चरमे जन्मनि यथा श्रीविद्योपासको भवेत् ।।

He alone is attuned with 'Shradha' in the 'Nama-kirtanam' of Sri Devi. The devotee becomes correspondingly the same Upasaka of Sri Vidya...,

76. नामसाहस्त्रपाठश्च तथा चरमजन्मनि ।
यथैव विरला लोके श्रीविद्यार्चनवेदिनः ।।

Who has done the 'patham' of 'Namasahasra' in the last birth. As the knowers of Sri Vidya happen to be very few in this world...,

77. तथैव विरला गुह्यनामसाहस्त्रपाठकाः ।
मन्त्रराजजपश्चैव चक्रराजार्चनं तथा ।।

So are very few, who recite the secret and highly occult Sahasranamas and also the japam of Mantraraja and the archana of Chakraraja.

78. रहस्यनामपाठश्च नाल्पस्य तपसः फलम् ।
अपठन् नामसाहस्त्रं प्रीणयेद्यो महेश्वरीम् ।।

The recital of this occult Sahasranama is not the merit of a little tapasya. He who recites this 'Namasahasra' without emotional attachment of Maheshvari....,

79. स चक्षुषा विना रूपं पश्येदेव विमूढधीः ।
रहस्यानामसाहस्त्रं न्यक्त्वा यः सिद्धिकामुकः ।।

Verily, he is a dull person, who is seeing the form without eyes. He who leaves the occult Sahasranama and is bent upon to have his desires fulfilled....,

80. यो भोजनं विना नूनं क्षुन्निवृत्तिमभीप्सति ।
यो भक्तो ललितादेव्याः स नित्यं कीर्तयेदिदम् ।।

Like a person, who wants to fill his stomach without taking any food in it. He is the sincere devotee of Lalita Devi, who makes the 'Kirtanam' regularly of the Mother-creatrix...,

81. नान्यथा प्रीयते देवी कल्पकोटिशतैरपि ।
तस्माद् रहस्यनामानि श्रीमातुः प्रयतः पठेत् ।।

Otherwise, so much of affection can never be had in the millions of 'Kalpas'. Therefore, the recital of the occult Sahasranama of Sri Mata – Mother Creatrix should be performed with care.

82. इति ते कथितं स्तोत्रं रहस्यं कुम्भसम्भव ।
नाविद्यावेदिने ब्रूयान्नाभक्ताय कदाचन ।।

O Kumbhasambhava Agastya! I have thus narrated you the Stotram with Rahasyam, being highly secret. It should not be imparted to any person ignorant of Sri Vidya and to any non-believer, in any circumstance...,

83. यथैव गोप्या श्रीविद्या तथा गोप्यमिदं मुने ।
पशुतुल्येषु न ब्रूयाज्जनेषु स्तोत्रमुत्तामम् ।।

As the knowledge of Sri Vidya is a secret one, so is the secret of this Supreme Stotram as well, O Muni! This Stotra should in no way be told to men, who are just like beasts in their nature and without discrimination.

84. यो ददाति विमूढात्मा श्रीविद्यारहिताय च ।
तस्मै कुप्यन्ति योगिन्यः सोऽनर्थः सुमहान् स्मृतः ।।

Any foolish person who gives the 'Rahasyanama - Sahasram' to any one, not been initiated into Sri Vidya is subjected to Kopa - displeasure of Yoginis and he suffers a lot.

85. रहस्यनामसाहस्रं तस्मात् सङ्गेपयेदिदमू ।
स्वतन्त्रेण मया नोक्तं तवापि कलशोद्भव ।।

This Sahasrama of occult nature, therefore must be learnt by heart O Kalashodbhava – Pot born Agastya! I have not narrated it to you of my own...,

86. ललिताप्रेरणादेव मयोक्तं स्तोत्रमुत्तमम्।
कीर्तनीयमिदं भक्त्या कुम्भयोने निरन्तरम्।
तेन तुष्टा महादेवी तवाभीष्टं प्रदास्यति।।

This Supreme efficacious Stotram has been narrated by me to you under the divine will of Sri Lalita. O of the lineage of Kumbha! Practise the Kirtanam regularly with devotion, and firm will. Thus Maha Devi will confer on you the best of results, you desire for.

श्रीसूत उवाच

Sri Suta Said

87. इत्युक्त्वा श्रीहयग्रीवो ध्यात्वा श्रीललिताम्बिकाम्।
आनन्दमग्नहृदयः सद्यः पुलकितोऽभवत्।।

Saying so, Sri Hayagriva meditated upon Sri Lalitambika. He got contented and felt in heart the ecstacy of Anandam-bliss, which is sypreme beautitude.

88. इति श्रीब्रह्माण्डपुराणे उत्तरखण्डे श्रीहयग्रीवागस्त्यसंवादे
श्रीललिता सहस्रनामस्तोत्रं नाम षट्त्रिंशोऽध्यायः।।

Here ends the epilogue of the thousand Names of Sri Lalitambika Sahasranama Stotram, during the discourse between Sri Hayagriva and Agastya Muni is the Uttarkhanda of Sri Brahmanda - Purana, forming the thirty-sixth chapter.

85